Driving Explosive Growth

A No Smoke and Mirrors Approach to Profitably Growing Your Business

Driving Explosive Growth

A No Smoke and Mirrors Approach to Profitably Growing Your Business

By

Mark Allen Roberts

To my mother and father,
who encouraged me to learn and taught me a work ethic through
their daily example.

To my wife Theresa,
who encouraged me to write this book, which was on my
heart for over 10 years to help me fill my dreams of serving others.

To my children,
Tyler and Jordan.

To Dr. Joy Schertley,
my executive coach for over 20 years, who gave me the courage to
find and develop my greatness to serve others.

Table of Contents

Introduction

"Do not succumb to the general panic. Think outside the box and look for a way out where nobody else expects to find it."
– Ryan Holiday

At any moment in time, six out of ten adults are thinking of starting a business. In the United States alone, an estimated 1,700 small businesses are started every day. That's 71 businesses per hour. Owning a business can provide financial stability and the flexibility that comes with being your own boss. The first problem is approximately 20% fail in the first year, 45% in the first five years, and 65% in the first ten years. Only 25% of new businesses make it fifteen years or longer. The second problem is, for those who are fortunate enough to survive any length of time, many become slaves in the day-to-day operations, and it can easily feel like their business owns them rather than being a business owner. Most don't realize every pitfall is avoidable when you start with the right foundation.

Even market-leading, billion-dollar organizations often struggle to scale their businesses. On average, businesses change market leadership positions every 10-12 years. If you don't believe me, let me ask you a few questions…

- In the last 3 months, how many movies have you rented from Blockbuster?
- In the last week, how many Yahoo searches have you done?
- How many of you use a Blackberry cell phone?
- In the last 30 days, how many of you have taken a roll of film to be developed?

Markets change and adjust to new buyer preferences and challenges all the time. Our businesses must constantly be sensing changes in our markets and trends to strategically pivot. Often business leaders face business challenges and how they solve them may surprise you. If you're a business leader, where do you turn when there's a problem in your business? If you're like anyone in the room full of CEOs I spoke to in Arizona, then your go-to option is probably phoning a friend – you know, someone in your business network or even a golf buddy you trust for wise counsel. But what if your friend isn't any smarter than you? Your second option may be talking it over with your spouse. After all, they have heard about your business for years and may even play a role in it. Another answer I heard from the group in Arizona was to go at it alone. It deeply concerns me that so many CEOs and entrepreneurs believe they are being paid to figure it out on their own. Then, the last option was to hire a consultant or coach.

The real irony here is that the last choice for helping their business would be the first choice in all other aspects of their lives. If they needed to improve their golf game, they would go to a pro. If they wanted to improve their physical fitness, they'd hire a trainer. If they were not feeling well physically, they would go to a medical professional. So, why aren't more business owners doing that for their businesses?

The assumption is that since your friend or spouse has heard you talking about your business at the breakfast table or dinner parties for the last thirty years, they must know something about it. Well, if you're a doctor and your spouse is a librarian, would you turn to them with questions about an upcoming surgery you need to perform? I didn't think so.

What we often find is they go at it alone, work harder, put in more hours, and lose the joy they once had. My passion is helping business leaders bring their joy back. The challenge is that the data many businesses are reviewing to build their strategy for growth is old, and they do not have access to the current market data, both from their customers and their transaction data. Their friends and spouse don't understand the skills of their team or any of the other seemingly small details that could make a big difference in achieving profitable growth for their organization.

In a survey of 2,700 CEOs, the number one thing keeping them up at night was the thought of there being a better, more effective, or more efficient way to do something but not knowing what it was. That really didn't come as a shock to me. When you look at the data, only 3% of companies right now are searching for somebody to help them. 97% are living in an environment where they believe they are stuck with the situation because it's always been this way. They're not actively researching what new solutions may be available. In my close to 40 years of sales and marketing leadership, I have seen it happen more times than I can count. The sad part is no one sets out to fail, and most don't even realize they are failing until the "going out of business" sign is hung in the window or their spouse of 22 years decides to leave them.

What if I were to show you the better way to scale your business and increase your market share, shareholder equity, and profits? Profitably growing an organization can be better than you ever imagined. There are steps you, as the owners of any size business, can take to assess the health of your operation and design an action plan based on those findings. We will share those steps and unpack each to help you and your team.

Ecclesiastes states, "There is nothing new under the sun." There are just new ways to apply thoughts, systems, and processes to solve new, urgent problems. As author Charles Swindoll shares, "Every new idea is an echo from the past." For over 30 years, I have read a book each week to seek out creative thoughts, models, processes, frameworks, and solutions and have saved those that resonated with me the most. I designed my business Out of the Box (OTB) Solutions in an effort to turn that knowledge into a means of helping thousands of business owners, just like you, implement my *No Smoke and Mirrors* process to scale their revenue to levels they never would have believed possible.

I have been blessed to read amazing books, attend seminars and workshops, and have conversations with gifted thought leaders in their disciplines – always searching for a better way to serve my clients and help make their visions and dreams come true. In fact, in all my years doing this, there is only one company I can think of where this *No Smoke and Mirrors* process didn't work, and in all honesty, that is only because they did not want to believe the data they were presented with.

No one ever wants to hear their baby is ugly, but when it comes to business, sometimes the painful truth is what needs to be told, understood, and accepted. If you are not getting to where you want to be but are unwilling to make any changes, then you're destined to stay stuck or, worse, go in reverse until the doors close for good. Einstein said, "Insanity is doing the same thing over and over again and expecting different results." In most cases, the teams I serve don't need to work *harder*; they need to work *smarter*, and they need to improve trust and communication. They need to understand the voice of their customers and market trends and write strategic growth plans based on the market of today.

I don't want your business to struggle or not grow, and I don't want you to experience the stress of downsizing or going out of business. If you follow the simple steps outlined in this book, the future can look drastically different – in a good way! But, numbers don't lie. You need to have thick skin and be receptive to the data. I always say, *"If you want to profitably grow your business, then hire a heretic."* As a man of faith, I know how that can sound, but at the end of the day, you need to hire someone who tells you what you *need* to hear and not what you *want* to hear. You need to have a culture of psychological safety and trust with team members who are free to have critical conversations and talk about things that matter to the business. After all, you are a smart business leader with industry knowledge and experience. If you and your team had the right actionable data, you could make the strategic pivots to drive repeatable profitable growth. Sometimes, it takes an outside, unbiased perspective to make these changes.

I don't claim to be the smartest person in the world or even in the room for that matter. If I can do this process, I promise you, anyone can do it. Over the years, I have probably made every mistake one can make in business – some, multiple times. I was not supposed to even go to college or be a business owner. When I was in first grade, the teacher met with my parents and told them I was "kind of slow," which was the appropriate way to say it back then. I had difficulty spelling and concentrating on my reading assignments, so they wanted to put me in the program for special needs kids, which in the 60s meant you sat out in the hallway so everyone knew you were slow.

With all of this pressure, I had no intentions of going to college. My plan was to join the United States Marine Corps and become a drill sergeant, which explains a lot if you worked with me in the early years. My high school guidance counselor and football coach suggested I take up a trade rather than go to college, but my parents pushed me to go, though I kept telling them I would barely pass. After graduating with a 2.75 GPA, I wasn't entirely wrong.

During my freshman year of college at Kent State University, I took a psychology course, and the professor told us the midterm exam would only consist of an essay. For me, that was great news since I had always done very well sharing my knowledge in essay format. But on the day of the test, a graduate assistant handed out the tests, and they were all multiple-choice questions, which I believe are only designed to see how well you can take a test rather than measure knowledge. Needless to say, I failed.

When the professor returned the following week, he distributed the tests throughout our classroom, a giant auditorium of over 300 students. I must have said something out loud when I saw my grade because the professor pointed to me, told me to stand up, and asked, "Do you have a problem you would like to share with the class?"

"Yeah, I got an F-ing problem," I said. "You told us to prepare for an essay, so I prepared for an essay, but you gave us a multiple-choice test, and I failed it. This is bullshit. I'm paying your salary, right? College is expensive, and this is not what I paid for!"

After my outburst, my classmates were shocked I had spoken to the professor that way, and he asked me to see him after class. When I went to see him in his office, he surprised me with an apology. "You're right," he said. "I had an illness in my family and didn't have the time to grade essay papers, so I changed it." He then asked me if I had a few minutes to talk and proceeded to ask me essay questions. I wrote my answers in

15

less than thirty minutes and got 100%. Intrigued, he wanted to know how easy it was for me to answer the questions. When I told him, he proceeded to have me take a number of assessments over the next few weeks.

It turns out, I am blessed with a skill he called "rapid pattern recognition." When most people see a jigsaw puzzle, they see thousands of tiny pieces and immediately start sorting similar pieces into piles. They look for puzzle pieces with a straight edge to start the frame, then they may pick a color or pattern to begin putting pieces together before moving on to another section. They look at the puzzle box image for guidance when they get stuck until they complete the full jigsaw puzzle.

However, people with rapid pattern recognition, like me, see the pieces in their minds and immediately put them together. When it comes to business situations, I see how the pieces connect, often in new ways, and how those connections can be applied. That was the first time I realized I had a gift – I just didn't know how I was going to use it in life. Eventually, I discovered I could apply this ability to help businesses by quickly identifying and putting all their puzzle pieces together in a way that drives *explosive* sales growth. This became my mission in life, as I help facilitate discussions that lead to strategic explosive growth plans.

Explosive growth is when your business grows at a pace of 30%, 40%, or 50% per year. Explosive growth often results in my clients doubling and tripling their revenue and net income in 2-3 years, with noticeable shifts in a year or less. The steps are simple, but the discipline to follow through on each is often hard. Because clients want to skip steps or deviate from the process, we often engage with them for 12-24 months. In our explosive growth process, our other deliverable is to design a sustainable system for you and your team, so you will no longer need my team in 2-3 years. It's not unusual for us to help our clients hire a VP of sales and marketing, COO, or CFO to lead their teams as we move to serve our next business owner.

Though businesses often face new challenges and constraints where we may be called in to fine-tune their systems and processes, the framework of the *No Smoke and Mirrors* process for explosive growth remains at the core. So many people in the business world are exaggerating or outright lying about doing whatever they need to do to achieve their goals, but achieving higher levels of success does not do anything fancy or deceitful. Actually serving people through authenticity and transparency, combined with a powerful system and process, is a much more effective way of getting to where you want to go.

We all have gifts, and I'm a big believer that we are all destined for greatness. The magic is finding where to use our gifts to provide the greatest value in serving others. I've used my gift for helping businesses grow profitably for just under 40 years now. I have easily worked with hundreds of companies that wanted to profitably grow but were stuck. I use all of the tools shared in this book to find the puzzle pieces for you, then group them together and recognize patterns so we can figure out what additional questions we need to answer. As I share with clients today, "There are dollars in your data if you know where to look." The problem is most companies just have too much data and are looking in the wrong places.

Most business owners don't plan to fail; they are just too close to the daily operations of the organization to have the building blocks or framework needed to succeed. I wish I could take the credit for "the founder's dilemma," a commonly used term for this situation, but I can't. A lot of founders follow the same trajectory – they have a great idea, which turns into a side hustle, then they grow the confidence and revenue to quit their day job and start a business. The problem is they often don't know the first thing about running a business. They launch and get traction quickly. It is easy to grow when your team has only 3-8 people. However, as you add more and more people to support the growth of your business, things change, and the business becomes more complex. Soon enough, all of the tasks they are not good at like operations, bookkeeping, and talent management cause them to hemorrhage cash, which is the reason 75% of businesses fail.

I recently ran into a case of this with a client who created a new product line of exhaust systems and bumpers for Jeep enthusiasts. While the founder was focusing on all of the exciting parts of the business, like creating advertisements, developing product designs, and stocking up on inventory to meet a future growth projection he and his buddy came up with on the golf course, I was making the case for putting in the difficult work needed for business development. There is always pushback when someone suggests putting in a lot of research and strategy work until you explain to them it will take an equal or greater amount of work to bankrupt their company by doing all the wrong things. It is always better to put in the research before making any expensive investments of time or money.

If this founder sounds like he has a lot in common with you, then please pay extra close attention throughout this book. From my experience, most business owners hate the minutia involved in keeping the lights on. They want to focus on what they were passionate enough about to start the business in the first place. They want to use their gifts in identifying and solving unresolved market problems, which is why I want to empower founders and business owners to do what they do best by fueling their love and passion to continue creating, designing, and innovating.

We are going to take a look at some of the ways you can start spending more time working *on* the business tasks you enjoy instead of toiling *in* your business while it spirals out of control. To do that, there needs to be a system, a process that helps business leaders grow their businesses and enjoy their families, friends, and other interests more. I promise it is not nearly as painful as you might think. There is nothing new under the sun, and learning from the mistakes and successes of others will help drastically reduce the learning curve.

Here is the *No Smoke and Mirrors* process that has helped hundreds, if not thousands, of companies:
1. **Assess**: We gather data to understand the current state and the desired future state.
2. **Collaborate**: Discuss the insights we have uncovered from the assessments and identify any gaps today that would prevent us

from achieving the desired future state. None of us are as smart as all of us working together.

3. **Prescribe**: We prescribe solutions to close the gaps. This is often strategy, training, coaching, new roles, systems, processes, tools, and technology.

4. **Communicate:** Clearly state the objectives, how we plan to achieve them, and by when. Each leader will then cascade these goals to each team member to ensure they understand how their behaviors and actions impact goal achievement.

5. **Plan**: Our team partners with the client's leadership team to create a one-page strategic plan, sales plan, marketing plan, engagement plan, operations plan, continuous learning plan, and financial modeling plan.

6. **Identify Key Performance Indicators (KPIs)**: We help teams focus more on leading than lagging indicators. We determine what we will measure, then we monitor those results weekly.

7. **Execute**: Implement the plan throughout the organization with a focus on outcomes more than actions. Here, we also focus on leadership, leadership alignment, and business culture in an environment of psychological safety.

8. **Adjust:** As we learn new information and gather new insights, we need to be agile and open to change.

9. **Improve Sales & Marketing Effectiveness:** Buyers have spoken, and they do not want reps. What they want and need today are business consultants. What will it take to help your sales and marketing team members become consultants?

10. **Strengthen the Core:** Hold all of the above steps together with the glue that connects team members – your culture, vision, and mission.

I will unpack each step for you, so you can read chapter by chapter, or you can isolate and focus on the chapter that may be new for your team when developing and executing business growth plans.

I'm sure this sounds like it is going to be a lot of work. I'm not going to lie to you – the process is simple, but it won't be easy. As Ray Dalio said in his book *Principles: Life and Work,* "If you don't evolve, you are slowly dying. Be open to new knowledge and new views of life, and don't be afraid to shoot for ambitious goals."

Before we can dive into the *No Smoke and Mirrors* process to drive explosive growth, we need to build a strong foundation in your company identity and within your sales team. Your company identity is your core – the glue that holds all your efforts together, and your sales team needs to perform based on human-to-human (H2H) selling. Sales often has a negative connotation, but H2H selling is an act of service, which is what I believe in and what I train salespeople to deliver.

Chapter 1: Company Identity

*"Excellence is never an accident. It is Always the result of high
intention, sincere effort, and intelligent execution; it represents the
wise choice of many alternatives choice not choice, determine your
destiny."*
– Aristotle

The core of what keeps everything together is your company's identity,
including your culture, mission, and values. A company cannot survive
– let alone thrive – if its identity is not clearly defined. Whether you
believe this or not, it is the glue holding everything together. If your
company was a person, what kind would you want it to be? Most people
do not spend nearly as much time on this question as they should. You
might think you have a clear mission, solid values, and a strong culture,
and you might be right on one or all of those points, but are they all
aligned and working together?

Company identity is the foundation of the success and growth of all
businesses. If you have been in business for a while, you might not have
the luxury of stopping everything you have going on to reassess these
pillars, but if you pay attention to each chapter of this book, you will be
in a much better position. Before we can even think about taking a deep
dive into your business, we need to start with the difficult task of
identifying exactly who you are as a company.

Without having your mission, vision, and values in place,
communicated, clearly understood, and reinforced, it is just a matter of
time before your team will struggle. It might be the loss of a large key
account, a change in senior leadership, or the stress of an economic
slowdown or recession. Maybe it will be when you receive a private
equity investment, and for the first time in your family business, you
now have a boss. Oftentimes, gaps arise when we complete strategic
acquisitions and need to share our culture. Whatever the stimulus, if you
do not invest time in your mission, vision, and culture strategically, it

will cause your business to stall at some point during your Scaling Up journey.

We must carefully consider our defining values and principles, our ultimate mission and vision, and the key elements that set us apart from our competitors. Only then can we construct a definitive portrait of our organizational culture that is both comprehensive and compelling, imbued with rich semantic nuances that convey our brand's identity and purpose.

I have consistently been called upon to assist companies in various industries with this challenge and found that each one, regardless of their sector or size, tends to believe they are uniquely different from others. I used to spend an inordinate amount of time trying to convince them otherwise; however, it became clear to me each company is, indeed, unique. From their mission and vision statements to their organizational culture and values, every business has its own distinct personality and set of team members within their leadership and throughout their organization that further sets them apart. Part of my role is to delve deeper into what makes each of my clients so unique in their own right.

Mission & Vision

"Make your life a mission - not an intermission."
– Arnold H. Glasgow

A lot of people use mission and vision interchangeably, when, in fact, they are distinct from one another. The mission is the purpose of the business while the vision is the aspiration of what the business wants to accomplish.

Your mission focuses on the why beyond your brand. When we help companies scale up, we refer to the mission as their purpose. Your mission defines what your organization is doing, what its objectives are, and how it will reach those objectives. Verne Harnish shares, "If the Core Values are the soul of the organization, the core Purpose (some call it mission) gives it its heart. This is what you do, why you do it, how you do it, and what value you consistently deliver." We think of our mission statement as a clear statement that helps our employees, customers, and the markets we serve know what we are about. As we work and facilitate leadership teams we ask the following question to help focus on a mission. What critical role does this team play in helping your customers, the markets, and the society you serve?

According to Stephen Covey, "If you don't set your goals based upon your Mission Statement, you may be climbing the ladder of success only to realize, when you get to the top, you are on the wrong building."

Examples of Mission Statements:

Apple
"Challenge the Status Quo."

Harley Davidson
"To fulfill dreams of personal, All-American freedom."

Disney
"To create happiness for people of all ages, everywhere."

Microsoft
"To empower every person and organization on the planet to achieve more."

From my experience, a mission statement should incorporate three parts: your purpose, your vision, and the value you create. Here is the template I like to use with my clients:

We (what you do) by (how you do it) for (your targeted ideal customers) to (value you deliver).

The mission statement for my business is:

We take a faith-based approach to serving business leaders who wish to scale revenue, profits, and shareholder value and help make their dreams of explosive growth and success come true.

Your mission statement is about who you are today. It becomes the foundation of your culture and helps guide your leadership team, employees, and stakeholders into alignment. It also guides strategic alliances and the vendors you chose to partner with.

A mission statement:
- creates the guardrails for all business procedures.
- helps to reinforce and grow a positive culture.
- highlights your distinctive competence, and what sets your brand apart from everyone else.
- attracts and retains customers, employees, vendors, stakeholders, and partners whose values align with yours.

On the other hand, vision is your ultimate *why*. When was the last time you thought about the vision for your business? I love to start with that question because I often find even those business owners, who started with a comprehensive vision for where they wanted to go, do not revisit it frequently enough to ensure it is still aligned with the current environment. The vision for growth is just the beginning, though. To stay aligned with that vision, you must also know why you want to obtain that level of growth and how it factors into the long-term vision of the company.

If you're the owner of the business, think about the loftiest goal you can imagine. Jim Collins refers to this as your BHAG (Big, Hairy, Audacious Goal). For some, the vision might be to grow to a point where you can go public and collect a big payout, while others could be creating something for their children and grandchildren to inherit and run for generations, which is my personal favorite. Or maybe you are just someone who likes to start businesses, and your vision is to sell the business in three to five years. All of these things play into what we do and how we will work together.

The world and business landscape have also changed significantly in recent years with much more emphasis being placed on issues unrelated to financial performance or reward. As business leaders, it is no longer enough to limit our vision to the traditional pursuit of profit and growth. Our vision needs to encompass a wide range of critical aspects, such as sustainability, social responsibility, and employee development. Job seekers now prioritize companies that actively invest in their people and the environment at large.

As a leader, it is important to not only focus on the quantifiable goals of revenue and EBITDA (earnings before interest, taxes, depreciation, and amortization) but also consider the impact your business has on the community it serves. Your vision should not solely revolve around personal success but should also involve the betterment of those around you. With this in mind, it is essential to prioritize the implementation of a diverse and inclusive workplace culture. By promoting equity and diversity in decision-making processes, companies can truly unlock the potential of every employee and pave the way for sustainable success.

Values

"Your principles have to reflect values you really believe in. By questioning all pre-packaged principles, you will be able to find the one you believe works best."
–Ray Dalio

Values are the rules of engagement for everyone working at your company. Many of my clients have faith-based values, which is great. They instantly resonate with me, and we are able to use those values as a measuring stick for what will or will not be acceptable. But you don't have to be a person of faith to apply values to the work your business does.

In the book *Built to Last*, authors Jim Collins and Jerry Porras make a strong case about how the best companies adhere to a set of principles they call core values. In the book *Scaling Up,* Verne Harnish shares how when you weave your values throughout the company, your leadership team will avoid getting sucked into many day-to-day operational issues. When an issue arises their first response will be, "Look at our core values, what do they suggest we do?"

In a Harvard Business Review article titled *"Make Your Values Mean Something,"* Patric Lencioni, author of the book *The 5 Dysfunctions of a Team*, challenges readers to consider if their values are doing more harm than good. Oftentimes, values can become bland toothless words, and he offers suggestions for how to make values meaningful.

First, we need to understand there are four different types of values:
- Core values: deeply ingrained principles that guide all our companies' actions. They serve as cultural cornerstones.
- Aspirational values: are necessary to succeed in the future but we currently lack them.
- Permission to play values: minimum behavioral and social standards required of an employee.
- Accidental values: these arise spontaneously without leadership input and take hold over time.

Confusing these values causes employees to grow frustrated and makes the senior leadership team look out of touch. Second, Lencioni suggests measuring their values by their content impact, not just randomly selecting four to five words to check off the values box. These values should be aggressively authentic to your company. Next, we can have value initiatives, which are about imposing a set of fundamental, strategically sound beliefs on a broad group of people. That's why the best efforts are driven by small groups. Lastly, we can weave our core values into everything. It's not something we just put on posters and share throughout the building. That's a start, but they must be integrated into all your systems, processes, and training. He compares our core values to fine wine, saying they take time and should not be rushed.

26

It is not unusual when I work with teams that we create a draft of their core values, but massage and wordsmith them over the next 3-4 months until they truly represent that company's identity. As we create and adjust these values, we consider if they are demonstrated by leadership, if they resonate with teams, if they are easy to understand, and if they are relevant to the employees' day-to-day.

Values are often a single word or two words. Some common ones are in this word cloud….

You don't have to get a fancy word cloud generator to put your values on paper though. This process starts from within, and it is likely your company will share many of the same values you hold personally. Take a few minutes to write down 5-10 words you feel are important in your life. If for any reason that is a struggle, we have also included a list of values for some well-known companies to help generate ideas.

Netflix
Netflix has a core philosophy of people over process. They define their corporate values as:
- Judgment
- Communication
- Curiosity

- Courage
- Passion
- Selflessness
- Innovation
- Inclusion
- Integrity

Apple

Apple values easy access to what they stand for as a company and lists its company values <u>on the footer of every page</u> of its website. These are:

- Accessibility
- Education
- Environment
- Inclusion and diversity
- Privacy
- Supplier responsibility
- Impact

My company's values are:

- Accountability
- Acts of service
- Trust
- Faith-based
- Integrity
- Innovation
- Continuous improvement

Culture

"Culture is simply a shared way of doing something with a passion."
– Brian Chesky

When mapping out the culture in your business, no one is restrained by the culture in place today. Even if there are culture gaps or items you would like to improve on, we can always make a plan to start shifting the status quo of "the way we've always done things around here." One of the biggest mistakes I made in helping a company grow was overlooking the fact that we didn't like each other when the engagement started. We grew the company rapidly. We brought on the team members to fill gaps as needed, but we didn't spend time designing our ideal culture. We did not invest in leadership team building or developing the trust required to scale.

This led to us having a team of very dysfunctional people who didn't trust each other and were each executing in their own silos. The culture was not what we originally designed or what we had when we launched the business. It just became that way over a long enough period of time as a result of no one actively addressing the little issues before they grew to be larger ones.

A strong commitment to diversity and inclusion is an essential factor that can make or break a company's appeal to top talent. By embracing these principles, companies can attract the best and brightest minds while nurturing and retaining their current talents for years to come. While building an inclusive and sustainable corporate culture gives companies a competitive advantage, it is also a morally and socially responsible choice that benefits everyone involved – from employees to customers to the planet as a whole. According to a recent analysis conducted by the Wall Street Journal, it has been revealed that the world's most profitable companies are those with diverse boards. This finding unequivocally confirms diversity plays a significant role in the success of a company and is so much more than a mere PR buzzword.

When we work with clients, we often spend half of a day with the senior leadership team to define the culture because it is so critical to explosive growth. When done right, it becomes a filter for how you do business and who you bring onto the team. Without that cultural fit, businesses can create more challenges and gaps for themselves. During a quarterly manager's meeting, we participated in a team-building exercise designed to evaluate which employees were embodying our company culture. Managers brought specific examples of these individuals to light and shared them with the team. Unfortunately, some teams had been falling short in communicating this recognition to their team members. When a manager identifies an employee as embodying the vision for teamwork, it is crucial to inform them of this observation. This communication is an essential step in the process of recognizing and rewarding the employees who are exemplifying our cultural values.

Recently, that company hosted a lavish dinner in Chicago. This wasn't just any ordinary dinner, but a carefully orchestrated affair aimed at reinforcing the company's culture and values to its attendees. During the dinner, the company awarded several of its top-performing employees who exemplified their core values. It was not just a mere plaque and handshake, but an in-depth sharing of each employee's story and how they demonstrated those values in their work. The entire event itself was an essential aspect of the company's culture, serving as a recognition of their employee's hard work and dedication as well as a means of promoting their core values to everyone present, which went miles in reinforcing the company's vision and mission.

Creating a cultural vision within a management meeting is a great first step, but this vision must then be implemented throughout the entire organization. This requires an active effort to ensure the vision is not only present but deeply ingrained within every aspect of the company. This same company was able to take up this challenge and consistently reinforce its culture in various ways, such as placing posters around the plant and creating a visually-appealing graphic to represent its values.

To further solidify their culture, they even designated a theme that embodies their core principles. Alongside these efforts, the company also recognized employees who best exemplified their culture on a frequent basis. If an employee acts in accordance with the company's five or six key cultural values, they are duly recognized. This reinforces the culture relentlessly and helps ensure the company's cultural vision is lived and breathed by all employees.

Alignment

"Building a visionary company requires one percent vision and 99 percent alignment."
– Jim Collins and Jerry Porra

The position of a CEO holds immense significance in shaping a company's identity, image, and success. To ensure the organization operates in line with its goals, we create a one-page strategic plan. This plan clearly defines the roles and responsibilities of every team member and specifies how each individual can contribute towards achieving objectives. Unfortunately, individuals often fail to dedicate adequate time and effort toward determining the means to attain their goals and understanding the underlying purpose of their goals.

The onus of strategically planning and envisioning falls upon the CEO, who is responsible for guiding the organization towards growth and progress. To effectively communicate and execute strategies, the CEO must over-communicate the plan to each member of the organization. Team members must understand the vision and mission of the company and be well-equipped to carry out their roles effectively. This will ultimately help the organization achieve its goals and establish a strong presence in the industry.

When I engage with clients and present ideas to them, they express their appreciation for the insight provided, which makes me believe it resonates with them. Yet sometimes, I am surprised to find that despite having shared the same idea multiple times, it is only truly resonating with them now because it has significance to them at the moment. As the CEO, it is crucial to instill this same discipline when communicating the company's vision, mission, and values to our employees. The process of achieving these objectives is equally, if not more, important than the objectives themselves. It is essential to constantly reinforce these values and objectives to ensure our employees remain on the path to success.

As a CEO at the beginning stages of a company, you have the advantage of intimately understanding all operations within the business. With a small staff, you maintain a close-knit relationship with every aspect of your organization, allowing you to quickly identify and address any issues that may arise. As a result, swift resolution is achieved with ease, providing you the opportunity to move forward with clarity and enthusiasm. As your business expands and matures, your responsibilities as CEO undergo a fundamental change. Rather than getting into the nitty-gritty of business operations, your focus becomes overseeing the enterprise and setting the course for its future.

Unfortunately, some individuals find it challenging to adapt to this new role. I've worked with several clients whose CEOs went back to performing hands-on duties, while I stepped in as CEO to ensure the business continued to run smoothly. It's not unusual for business leaders to struggle with the transition from doer to overseer, but there are ways to make it easier. There's a natural progression of business growth, and it's important to recognize the role of the CEO is bound to change as well. By being proactive and having a clear understanding of what's needed, any CEO can make the shift to an overseeing and visionary position.

Building and growing a successful business involves various phases and strategies. The journey starts with the launch of your company, typically as a sole proprietor or freelancer. At this point, you're flying solo, and it's up to you to steer the ship toward success. However, as your business begins to take off, you'll need to start assembling a team of competent and culturally-aligned individuals who can help you scale your operation. When hiring support staff, it's critical to prioritize competence and cultural fit to ensure your team shares your vision and values. Often, business owners tend to hire friends and acquaintances who they've known for years and can trust because they are often more likely to understand the nuances of the founder's business model and work ethic, making them an ideal fit.

As your company grows, your hiring needs will become more diverse, and you'll need to bring in a more diverse range of talent. Ideally, you'll want to avoid tunnel vision and expand your hiring horizons to include more qualified candidates who can contribute to the company's continued success. Eventually, you may need to pivot and launch new products or services to remain relevant and competitive. The process of plateauing and launching anew is a continuous cycle that requires both creativity and strategic vision to execute successfully.

Building a successful business will require a blend of hard work, perseverance, and the ability to pivot and adapt to changing circumstances. By assembling a team of competent, culturally-aligned individuals, you'll be able to build a company that can weather any storm and continues to thrive over the long haul. That's why you need to succinctly communicate your expectations for values and culture within the company. However, being a good CEO involves more than just stating expectations. It also involves ensuring the entire leadership team has a say in the direction the company is heading.

When we evaluate the value of a business, particularly if the business is set to be sold or bought, we like to ask how many hours the CEO in question works per day or per week. CEOs often pride themselves on working up to 15 hours a day. However, businesses with a CEO who can work just 15 hours a week are far more valuable than those with a CEO who has to clock in 15 hours a day. A CEO who spends a mere 15 hours at work per week, has likely invested their time and energy wisely in developing, innovating, and simplifying company systems and processes. They handpicked a talented workforce equipped and motivated to make the business thrive. Working fewer hours indicates the CEO has put in the hard work of creating efficient systems and processes and hiring the best possible talent to enable the smooth running and scalable growth of the business.

A company led by such a capable CEO is not only adept at coping with the daily demands of an always-changing market, but it is also readily scalable into the global arena. In contrast, a CEO who works crazy hours daily with no vision for delegation and employee growth is a factor that devalues the enterprise. When we consider purchasing a business, the last thing we want to see is a CEO who runs and controls the business single-handedly. It begs the question of what happens to the business when the CEO leaves or retires. Naturally, we don't want to buy a business where the departure of the current CEO will result in the business falling apart, so it's best to invest in a business with an efficient team and process that is scalable and sustainable in the long run.

When one of my clients was 67, he faced a pivotal moment as his wife approached him and expressed her desire for him to consider retirement within the next year. When someone plans to retire, it's best to begin implementing a strategic plan at least three years prior to ensure a smooth transition and maximize the value of his business. This process involves carefully assessing its strengths and weaknesses, identifying areas for improvement, and capitalizing on opportunities to increase profitability. Potential exit strategies may include transferring ownership to family members such as children or grandchildren, which is a popular option for many of my clients. In these cases, the goal is to create a lasting legacy for future generations, which requires a strong, sustainable business model that can withstand the test of time. Others want to sell their business and use the money for their retirement. Either way, the best time to start optimizing a business's value is three years before the intended sale date. Another option is to take your company public. Alternatively, employees might consider buying out your business, which is currently a trend in the industry.

No matter what, the exit path you choose should align with your ultimate goal. Here are the steps you will need to take to make sure your exit strategy is in alignment:
- consider your objectives.
- examine the business's financial performance.
- study market trends and competitors.
- create a well-defined exit strategy that caters to your individual needs.

That way, as the CEO, you can work to devise an exit plan that will meet your desired outcome and benefit the sustainability and growth of your business.

During my conversations with CEOs, we frequently discuss exit strategy, yet I'm always surprised by how often CEOs express uncertainty or ignorance toward this idea. As a business leader, it is vital to have a clear plan and direction for the future of your company. Failing to do so means risking the longevity and success of your business.

Several unforeseen events may arise during your business journey, such as a divorce, debt, or even bankruptcy. These situations can seriously affect your company's stability and growth. As a CEO, it is your responsibility to create a solid foundation for your business that can withstand any potential disruptions and remain in alignment. With the right team in place with the right skills, a clear and shared vision, and strong company values and processes, you can create an "umbrella of safety" to protect your business from unexpected obstacles and navigate through any uncertainties. This approach will also allow you to maintain a healthy work-life balance, avoiding the burnout that plagues many CEOs. As a result, you will be able to provide better leadership to your team, achieve sustainable success for your organization, and help create the identity you always wanted.

One of the most common situations we are seeing today is where an owner who had the vision to scale the business and leave it to the children and grandchildren, but none of them want the business. If you want to plan for a liquidation event and make your entire family very wealthy, then the time to start working on selling your business is three years before you want to sell it. If your vision is to go public, then what we really need to do is tighten up your market share, your EBITDA, ideally EBITDA by employee, and improve the efficiency and effectiveness of your business to increase shareholder value.

We want to ensure you are delivering repeatable sales with your customers year over year and your revenue and gross profit are growing as well. When trying to scale revenue, we often find companies compromise their value, and their gross margins decline. We do not want this for our clients and, with some strategic pricing and net profit by customer analysis, can often make the necessary corrections in 3-6 months. Our advice is not to let this happen in the first place by pricing your product or service based on the value it delivers to your customers rather than your cost to produce.

If your EBITDA is not strong, let's say in the 4% - 7% range, we need to work on increasing it long before you ever start entertaining purchase offers. Some of the owners we work with are shocked when somebody makes an offer for their business that's significantly less than what they would have dreamed, and that's when their *blood, sweat, and tears* all those years were really not getting a return on investment. That's why the time for them to improve their EBITDA is three years before they want to sell it. In that window, you need to work on putting in place robust systems and processes to go along with EBITDA so a new owner does not feel like you are your business.

If selling the business is a top priority, here are some questions certified Scaling Up coaches ask to establish potential value:
1. Is the entrepreneur/owner working 7 days per week for 15 hours a day, or are they working 15 hours per week?
2. Does the leadership team have scheduled meetings throughout the year to discuss a strategic plan?
3. Is your customer base diversified, or does one of your customers represent 60% of your business?
4. Do you have recurring, predictable revenue, the same customers buying for years, or rollercoaster revenues?
5. Are there documented systems, and does your team follow them?
6. Do you set and track company and department key performance indicators (KPIs)?
7. Is your profitability increasing as your revenue grows?
8. Are your critical performance statistics communicated and visible for all to see?

Buyers and investors in businesses look for the answers to these questions and more. How prepared is your team to answer them?

Chapter 2: Human-to-Human Sales

"Along with being concerned about return on shareholder value, the company strives to achieve sales and asset growth. Being a market leader, General Motors makes sure it honors its commitments to employees, clients, dealers, suppliers and the community."
– Alfred Sloan

Before we can even get into the *No Smoke and Mirrors* process and all the ways it can be used to drive explosive growth in your business, we must first cover the misconception of what sales really is. With your company's identity clearly defined, it will be easier to see why it's so important to treat our customers well.

I have been in sales for almost 40 years, but I haven't sold to anyone in 30 years. You might think that's concerning considering this entire book is about explosive growth through sales, but what I actually do is help people buy. I help them fix problems, and I've closed millions of dollars of business doing that. Selling is the ultimate act of service. For whatever reason, I'm seeing many salespeople have stopped having human-to-human conversations. They jump right into the pitch, and their close rates are terrible because they fail to build rapport, which is the second step of the sales process. So, I've been spending a lot of time teaching the basics to salespeople.

With everything going on in this world today, some salespeople have confided they don't feel comfortable selling because people are dealing with some pretty challenging circumstances. This is where I was able to jump in and help reframe their mindset. I asked if their customers had more or less problems now than they did a few years ago. Most agreed they had more. Then I asked, "Can you help them?"

I always coach salespeople to stop selling and start helping. When you can reframe the mindset of your salespeople to "How can I help this person?" instead of "How do I sell to this person?" magic happens. I've had clients contact me weeks later and tell me their sales have been better, which has made their relationships and overall well-being better.

In sales, we often talk about B2B or C2C, but selling is really about H2H (human-to-human), no matter what type of sales you're doing. Sales is not just about acquiring new accounts, placing new orders for existing accounts, or gaining your unfair share of the customer's spending wallet. Although, if you aren't trying to capture more, I assure you, your competition is, and they will not feel bad if there is less left for you. Sales being the ultimate act of service is the heart of my business. We seek to help our current customers identify challenges and solve problems because helping our clients succeed delivers more value to their bottom lines.

When we talk to our key contacts, we can see just how much their lives have improved. We create business relationships based on trust, and our goal is to be seen as a trusted advisor, not just another rep trying to hit an arbitrary quota set by a leader or manager. Working with clients, we often find what they want and need is often much different than the last client we helped. Everyone has their own unique problems, and in order to understand that and know how to help them, we need to have a human-to-human sales conversation.

To give you a quick example of the wrong way to sell, let's look at a medical device manufacturer I've worked with. Their goal was to grow 40% per year over the next six years and be acquired by a larger medical device company. Many companies will go out, buy a list, divide it among the salesforce, and say, "Go get them!" The people with skills will show some traction, but most of the team will struggle. Then, they end up going back to their current customers in the quiet of the night to sell more to them because, quite frankly, it's easier and they can get their commissions flowing again.

What went wrong? The sad reality is 50% of salespeople have never been trained in sales skills. When it comes to selling new business, the biggest mistake most people make is they take a huge list and just start dialing for dollars. They don't have the systems, the processes, the tools, or the value-based messaging for different customers. They're basically creating a bunch of interruptions for people who probably could become customers if approached correctly.

If you want to improve the overall sales effectiveness of your team, training is just one small piece of the overarching sales skillset. This is why you'll need to evaluate your sales team to see what skills they possess and which ones they need to improve on. When we look at sales skills, there are about 10-12 key skills required of salespeople today.

What I'm finding today is quite a few salespeople are very knowledgeable about their products, their services, and maybe even the applications of their products, but where they struggle is having conversations that ultimately turn to revenue. When we start reaching out, we want to avoid selling and start serving. Sales is about understanding the other person. Sales is about caring for other people, truly seeking to understand, and helping them.

This requires us to understand the needs of various personas and speak the language of their business. Your customers do not talk about your features and benefits in their weekly meetings. They discuss topics like increasing profits, reducing costs, improving cash flow, and increasing shareholder value. Human-to-human selling is about understanding your customers, what is important to them, and helping to connect your product or service as a means to achieving their desired outcomes.

Growth Strategies

"Strength and growth come only through continuous effort and struggle."
–Napoleon Hill

When we work with clients, we take the same human-to-human approach we use when training salespeople. A lot of people like to mention growth and how they want to grow, but we've found people tend to define growth very differently. People are interested in growing in a variety of ways such as: sales, revenue, net income, EBITDA, headcount, building capacity, skills, systems, processes, and the list goes on. There are a lot of different ways to grow, but not all growth is created equal. We are going to focus on growing your sales profitably.

We start off by identifying the current state. We look at what your sales have been over the last 36 months and determine if they have met your key objectives. Although it might come as a surprise, according to InsideSales, most teams haven't met their key objectives, so if your team is not achieving your growth goals, you're not alone. It's important to note where you are in your business on the day we start, so we can compare the results on how far we've come.

Once we fully understand the current state, we can identify what your objectives are. I want you to really sit and define growth. Is the growth going to come from current or new customers? Is it going to come from new products? Launching internationally? At this juncture, a lot of people talk about upselling, cross-selling, and increasing their share of their customers' wallets. Those are all needs to be considered when it comes to increasing your sales, but it's also important for us to understand *when*. In what timeframe would you like to achieve those results?

I had a client reach out to me who expressed their business was stalled at approximately $15 million for the last five years, and they wanted to grow to $30 million. Their solution was to hire me to provide training and coaching to fix the problem within 2-3 months. At that point, I had to explain it's a much longer process, and we were looking at 12-18 months to build the foundation, move through the process, and have the long-term impact the CEO desired. He later hired me to do it, and his team is going through the process as I write this. The point is, quality and sustainable growth takes time.

We like to have realistic conversations with our clients because, ultimately, there are many different strategies to drive sales growth. We can grow sales through:

- Current customers, which involves increasing the size of current accounts.
- New customers in our current markets.
- New accounts in the different markets where we know people value us.
- New products, which is an area quite a few teams really struggle with.
- New sales from new products to new customers.

The last bullet point is the most challenging for teams, but ironically, this is where most teams spend most of their time. It's more expensive and more time-consuming than any other sales behavior you can do. We recently completed market research for a very large trade association, where we contacted over 300 manufacturers. We expected to hear their biggest constraint was labor, supply chain challenges, and things like that, but their number one issue was consistently identifying, having conversations with, and closing new business.

Another sales approach is to sell more to your key accounts. Here, we collaborate with our key clients. We understand what their goals are and what the impact on their net income will be when achieving these goals, then we share ways we can help them. We develop account growth plans and we revisit them quarterly. The key account growth plans could be a book of its own, but if you want to learn more about developing key account growth plans you can use the QR code on Page 161 to check out my website where I have over 12 articles on what a key account growth plan must include.

After you've determined what kind of growth you can get with your current customers, you can compare it to what kind of growth you can get from other customers in the same market verticals, just in new locations. If that doesn't meet the requirements your shareholders want for growth, then we need to sell the same products to new customers, often in new verticals.

Value Proposition & Prospecting

"Consistent alignment of capabilities and internal processes with the customer value proposition is the core of any strategy execution."
– Robert S. Kaplan

Without a purpose or the ability to differentiate yourself from everyone else who calls on a prospect and key current clients, all you've done is interrupted them, failed to deliver any value, and left them wondering what problems you solve and how you could serve them. One of the best places to establish the value you can provide is on the initial outreach, even if it is just a voicemail. Before making any phone call, you need to have a pre-prepared, crisp value message you can deliver to the prospect to increase the odds of a callback.

Author Shanelle Mullin shares how value propositions should meet three criteria:
- Specific: What are the specific benefits your target customer will receive?
- Pain-focused: How will your product fix the customer's problem or improve their life?
- Exclusive: How is it both desirable and exclusive? How well does it highlight your competitive advantage and set you apart from competitors?

When you first reach out to prospective buyers, over 80% of your conversations will be with their voicemail, so make sure you feel very confident in sharing your value proposition in a short amount of time. If this is an area where you struggle, we have a template for voicemail best practices available by using the QR code at the end of the book. Your value proposition is the foundation of your sales process, so you need to understand your why, and make sure your entire organization understands it.

Once you have solidified your value proposition, you can create a sales plan to begin prospecting. While I train and coach teams to have a prospecting cadence, we make the cadence unique to each company based on insights from their CRM, our Voice of Customer assessment data, and conversations with their salespeople. Today, it is not unusual to have to contact customers 20 times before having a conversation. From the data produced by our OMG sales effectiveness assessment, most salespeople quit after 2-3 attempts and buyers engage after 12-20 attempts. Your probability of success grows exponentially after 20 attempts. If the contact does not engage after 25 touches, I advise clients to put their contact into a lead nurture campaign until marketing identifies them as a qualified lead based on their behavior. Some behaviors we monitor are the open rate of messages, the click-through on links, the download of content, attending a webinar, and so on.

If you do not have a formal and continuous prospecting cadence, you will experience rollercoaster revenue. One month, the sales team sales will hit their goals, but the next month or two, you won't see any new customers, resulting in missed sales plans. We want and need sales prospecting continuously. When you build your cadence, keep in mind all the ways you can contact customers today. You will monitor the response from each message and adjust your cadence as you see patterns. Your salespeople will work with marketing and log each customer contact in the CRM, so they can see patterns and trends on what was successful and what can be improved.

Some of the touchpoints include:
- Phone call (my favorite and too few people use it)
- Email
- Text
- Voice-recorded text
- Direct mail
- LinkedIn connection
- LinkedIn message
- Connect or message on other social platforms
- Face-to-face meeting
- Zoom meeting
- Send an email with something valuable to the other person (another one of my favorites)
- Trade shows

- "Contact Us" page or form on their website
- Trade association events
- Webinar invitation
- Send a video
- Send blog posts

Since every prospect is different, there is no right or wrong combination of contact methods, but the first step is always a phone call. You should expect to leave a voicemail, then send an email right after the voicemail explaining why you were calling. 24 hours later, make another phone call. Then, follow up on LinkedIn by asking to connect or sending the person a message. If none of those touchpoints work, send the person an email with something of value for their industry or their role. Follow up with another phone call.

Prospecting needs to be done continuously. Even if your sales pipeline is full, you need to have a prospecting cadence where people are always out there looking for new business with current customers, as well as new customers. You will need to put in the work, track the results, and determine which strategy works best for you.

A lot of salespeople blow it because the customer wasn't expecting the call, and it comes across as an ambush, especially if the person is in the middle of something. When that's the case, I always coach salespeople to say, "I know you weren't expecting my call. Do you have 30 seconds to hear how I help leaders like you?" Then, they should ask to schedule a 20-minute call at a better time in the future. If they say yes, you can continue with, "Do you have your calendar in front of you?" I learned this discussion model from Chris Beall, CEO of Connect and Sell, who delivered an amazing workshop at an AAISP conference.

It's a simple process and very unobtrusive, but you must be realistic. If you have a list of 350 people, you'd be lucky to have six quality conversations in your first round of contacts. You will need to be prepared. Don't try to wing it or "show up and throw up," hoping something you say resonates with the other person.

We always recommend knowing and starting with your ideal customer profile. When I used to have my own sales teams, I asked them what they knew about the client, their market, and, more importantly, how they make money. Then, we target the potential clients who have the highest potential for your salespeople to close and equip your salespeople with a really strong, tight value proposition that makes people want to engage.

When we work with sales teams, we provide them with a simple checklist, similar to a pilot's preflight checklist. On a flight, you might notice the pilot and the flight attendants walking around the plane before takeoff to make sure they are prepared for the flight ahead. You can find a copy of my sales preflight checklist using the QR code on Page 161, where I list various items you should consider before you make the call so you can give your prospective customer the best experience.

Conversations That Lead to Revenue

"We don't have to engage in grand, heroic actions to participate in change. Small acts, when multiplied by millions of people, can transform the world."
– Howard Zinn

The most significant factor of human-to-human (H2H) sales is having conversations that lead to revenue. The course I teach on this, aptly called Conversations that Lead to Revenue, is based on 9 easy-to-follow steps. The upcoming steps are very detailed and should be followed without deviation, whenever possible, to ensure a successful sales call.

#1 Ideal Customer Profiles

"An ideal customer profile is based on company level firmographic and technographic data points (like employee size, technologies used, industry, and more), and it serves as a representation of your ideal customer."
– Hubspot

The first thing we have to do is identify what our ideal customer profile is. Far too many new clients have what they refer to as "target opportunity lists" that lack the discipline of identifying their ideal customers. One way to identify ideal customers is to analyze the net profit of current customers, establish which are most profitable, then find and strategically win more clients fitting that profile. When we look at what all those customers who really value us have in common, including what we are selling them and what markets they are in, we will typically find a few new markets we may not be focusing on but are contributing a lot of value to our bottom line. It's important to understand the ideal customer's revenue, employee headcount, current markets, the biggest factors in their buying decisions, and key stakeholders.

One of my clients is a manufacturer of products used in oil and gas refineries. They are experiencing growth, but their owners wanted to see repeatable growth greater than 20% year-over-year. We reviewed their transaction data and their net profit by customer data and noticed a few new account names in their top 20 accounts in terms of revenue and net profit. We reached out to these firms and found one thing in common – they were selling my client's products to paper and pulp manufacturing facilities. In our interviews, we learned my clients' products were a perfect solution for a problem these facilities have struggled with for years.

We captured how they described this problem in the language of their industry, identified the decision makers who were typically tasked with solving this problem, and interviewed them to clearly identify their business drivers. We then shared the keywords and phrases with our

46

web SEO partner, who then developed landing pages and brochures that explained the problem, how we solve it, and the economic impact customers in this industry were experiencing using my client's products. We developed an ideal customer list for the paper and pulp manufacturing market and trained our independent sales representatives on our value proposition for this market and persona-based messaging for each decision maker our interviews identified. In 2022, this product line grew over $3 million dollars, and our plan for 2023 is over $7 million.

We focus on peeling back the metaphoric onion to discover the layers that constitute what a good customer is for us. Sometimes, we can do it by market vertical. We can do it by the size of the business, revenue, number of employees, markets they serve, or physical products versus service products. A lot of different things will ultimately bubble to the surface after you look at the data.

According to Hubspot, defining your ideal customer profile will allow you to:
- Focus your efforts, time, and investments on customers with higher possibilities to buy your product or service.
- Help your salespeople to avoid spending valuable selling time on accounts that will not buy.
- Limit the accounts your team will focus on. You can filter the leads using buying signals, trigger events, and improve the volume and quality of your leads.
- Align your marketing and messaging to improve your ROI in marketing investments.

Then, we build our target list strategically and identify the key decision makers who we learned have the power to make the buying decision and influence purchases. A lot of teams make a mistake here by buying a list from a lead generation or data mining company, so to save you the time and money of going down that road, there is an ideal customer worksheet download for free using the QR code on Page 161.

#2 Rapport

"Rapport is the ultimate tool for producing results with other people. No matter what you want in your life, if you can develop rapport with the right people, you'll be able to fill their needs, and they will be able to fill yours."
– Tony Robbins

One of the biggest challenges I experience coaching salespeople since the pandemic is their rapport-building skills. If you were meeting with a client face to face, it's easier to build rapport with them. Though building rapport is key to developing relationships and lifetime customers, since the pandemic, the art of building rapport has been replaced by what I refer to as "pitch slapping" your customers. Pitch slapping is assuming you know what the client's challenges are and the impact they have on their business, then pitching to them without building any rapport or asking discovery or qualifying questions.

Is it just me, or do pitch slapping salespeople always call at dinnertime? You know the scenario – you just sat down to dinner, your phone rings, and you see a local number. You pick it up thinking it may be someone you know, but immediately some poorly trained salesperson begins trying to sell you internet service, new cell phone service, windows, or doors. If this hasn't happened to you, maybe you've experienced the modern-day version of pitch slapping on LinkedIn when you log in to find a message from one of your new connections who politely thanks you for the connection, introduces themselves, and immediately starts telling you about what they think you need and how they can help you get it.

As more and more sales activities move to a hybrid model, we need to make sure our salespeople have the skills to naturally build rapport throughout a conversation. Sometimes, this requires doing some homework before even starting a conversation. One of my recommendations is for salespeople to check the LinkedIn profile of the person they are reaching out to to find out where the person worked before, where they went to school, and if they have any common connections.

If you are meeting a total stranger and you did your homework, the interaction might sound something like this:

> "Hey, I saw your LinkedIn profile. We both served in the same industry, and we both went to Kent State. I'd just like to have a quick conversation."

When we train salespeople, we train them how to build rapport on a cold call by letting the customer set the tone for the relationship. We are starting a conversation but always keeping it open enough to let the customer decide how much rapport they want and need. If they reply, "Yes, it was great! What year did you go to Kent?" then that's wonderful. If they quickly say, "Look, I've only got 10 minutes, what's the purpose of this call?" then they really don't want to establish rapport, and we need to honor what they want.

Once they want to engage, we recommend your next question be, "Do you have your calendar in front of you? When can we have a conversation?" Always be prepared to suggest some dates and times. Typically, one of two things is going to happen here:
- They might check their calendar and give you some dates.
- They might ask you to get to the point and say something like, "I'm busy. What's this call about?"

Typically, what I'll say to the second response is:

> "Over the last 30+ years, I've learned you can't have a really good conversation in 3-7 minutes. I'm asking if you could give me 15-20 minutes on a future date, and I might be able to provide some insights on ways I can help you."

Usually, they will agree to set a scheduled date in the future. If you ask a few questions and the client wants to talk, then keep talking. If the client says something like, "I only have 20 minutes," then respect their desire not to spend time building rapport and move to discovery.

When you are building rapport and they are willing to have a conversation, keep in mind that people buy from people. You hear a lot about sales, sales techniques, B2B, and B2C, but it's really all about H2H interactions. They will make a decision within the first 4-7 seconds on whether or not they can trust you and if they think you can help them. Then they'll validate that belief throughout the rest of your conversation. This is why the rapport phase is crucial and why pitch slapping will get you nowhere.

If you are still struggling to determine the best rapport building questions, a comprehensive list of possible questions can be found using the QR code on Page 161.

#3 Discovery

"Approach each customer with the idea of helping him or her to solve a problem or achieve a goal, not of selling a product or service."
– Brian Tracy

We use the discovery phase to determine if a customer has problems we can solve. This is the meeting we asked to schedule, and we ask questions to better understand their current state and desired future state. Then, we have to determine if the problems they share with us match the products and services we offer. Warning – from my research, only 3% of customers are actively searching for solutions to problems they are aware of. That leaves many who have problems but do not believe there is a solution to solve them, and some may not be aware of the problem or the root cause to begin with.

By the nature of your questions, you can demonstrate competence and build trust. Discovery questions should be open-ended, meaning they cannot be answered with a yes or no, because we want the customer to talk. As a general rule, when I coach salespeople, we want the customer to talk 70% of the time. When we teach our course on conversations that lead to revenue, we ask the trainees to develop their own questions in their own language. No one likes to have a script read to them, so please make some of the below questions your own. As a reminder, buyers buy based on trust and the seller's competence, which you can establish by the very nature of your questions.

When we work with CEOs, we break up the open-ended questions with "Could it be" conversations to troubleshoot why a team feels stuck and isn't growing. These are technically closed-ended questions, but they are deeply thought-provoking. When I ask these questions, I realize this is often the first time the leaders have been asked them:

- Could it be your sales team isn't trained?
- Could it be you have some quality issues?
- Could it be your production plant is unable to execute on time?
- Could it be your salespeople need to improve their virtual selling skills?

For more discovery questions, please see the QR code on Page 161.

Say you're calling plastic injection molders. You know your market, so you know some people like them are struggling with resin prices. In this case, you might have a discovery question such as, "How is your team dealing with the rising cost of resin?" Pause and wait for the prospect to respond. The goal is to have the prospect talking around 70% of the time, so make sure to let them talk. Then you can say, "A lot of our clients in this industry are also seeing challenges with resin, and here's how we help them (fill in the blank for how you help your customers)."

We recommend you have two or three really good discovery questions, so you can find out if they have any problems you can solve. If the answer is no, then you can end the whole engagement very quickly. Although this might seem like you're giving up, you're actually doing yourself a favor. By getting to know if they need you as fast as possible, you can spend your time with the buyers who need you most.

#4 Qualify

"If you are not moving closer to what you want in sales (or life), you probably aren't doing enough asking."
– Jack Canfield

If we find they do have challenges we can solve, then we qualify them. IBM created a system in the 1980s referred to as BANT: budget, authority, need, and timeline. It's important to understand each of these and ask these questions in a polite way. Many salespeople are afraid to ask questions because they're worried about hurting the relationship, but there is always a way to ask politely. When we conduct the OMG sales effectiveness and improvement analysis, we often discover salespeople score very high in the need to be liked, but top-performing salespeople need to be respected, not liked.

The goal is to understand if the customer has a budget, but the salesperson is often so concerned about being liked that they skip this step because they feel it's intrusive. However, it's actually doing you and the customer a big favor. It's all about how you ask. You could be very direct and say, "Do you have a budget for this project?" Or, you could ask it a lot softer by saying, "Usually, when I work with clients at this stage, they either have a budget or they ask me to help them build a budget. Do either of those apply to you?"

You are going to find people who have a lot of problems, but they don't have the funds to pay for the solutions. Some thought leaders criticize BANT because we may disqualify someone who could have found a budget if we presented a compelling enough business case. Business cases can be used if we feel the opportunity is great enough, and we believe we can help them find the funds. Here, we use success stories from other clients we have served like them and emotionally connect them to achieving similar, if not greater, outcomes.

In addition to a budget, we also need to establish if they have authority. When we do sales assessments, we often find salespeople are not talking to the decision maker. If the person we are speaking to does not have the authority to enter into an agreement, we need to find the right person as quickly as possible and invite them into the conversation. If you're talking to the wrong person, you're not going to make a sale.

One way to establish authority is to say, "Lately, we've discovered there are quite a few people involved in buying decisions. Do you see that at your company as well? Is there anybody else we should involve in this conversation?" That's a very soft, professional question to ask.

Then, there's the need. If we don't understand the need our client has, we really need to dig deeper. There's a concept called the Iceberg Principle, which is a theory that most buyers and decision makers will only tell you what you can see above the water, but what gets you their business is finding what's below the water line, which requires asking probing questions that other reps haven't asked. While assessing needs, confirm what they listed as their problems. Ask, "Could it be X causing this problem?" Then, let them speak. A lot of people will discuss their problem, but they don't realize the problem is only a symptom of another problem. If we only fix symptoms, we are never going to create the impact we need. This is why we need to dig deeper and ask questions such as:
- How does that impact your bottom line?
- What is the impact of not solving this problem?
- How long has that been a problem?"

No matter what you ask, it's important to find out what they've done so far to try to solve that problem.

Last but not least, we have the timeline. When I was leading sales teams, it drove me crazy when a rep came back from a client meeting, told me they had an awesome meeting, and gave me all the information they gathered, but failed to get a timeline. When I asked, "When does the customer need it?," there were crickets. We need to understand their timeline so we can deliver what they need *when* they need it.

Salespeople can waste a lot of time, energy, and resources chasing business they can never win. It's key to focus on calling on people who would value you most. In discovery, we find out if they have problems we can solve. In qualifying, we determine if they have problems they are willing to pay to get solved, when they need them solved, and ideally the economic impact of not solving them. In this stage, we need to make sure we are talking to a decision maker.

#5 Propose Solutions

"Solution selling is designed to help sellers understand and align with how buyers buy."
– Keith M Eades

When talking to potential customers, many salespeople want to jump to proposing solutions with the belief that their product or service can solve all of the customer's problems. That's not always the case though. Once we've gone through steps 1-4, we want to review some of the things we've discussed with the customers and make sure we have a clear understanding of their problem. We must connect the dots between solving the problems for the client and the economic impact, so it's important to collaborate during this step.

This is where I advise salespeople to pause and take a step back. The majority of people don't come up with the best solutions on the fly. I tend to say, "Let me spend some time on this and get back to you with some ideas to help you meet your objectives. Are you available on ___?" Then, I give them a date, typically no later than two days.

Though you might think this goes against the very nature of everything you know about sales, taking a step back to gather information, discuss solutions with peers, and collaborate to find the best solution for the customer will put you ahead of other competitors in your customer's mind. Rather than rushing into the sale to get their money as quickly as possible, this shows them you truly care about trying to solve their problem. Then, when you have that meeting with the customer two days later, you can ask important questions to come to a unique solution.

If you use the QR code on Page 161 you can access the questions we teach our clients to use. If you begin practicing these questions, you will have conversations that lead to revenue. My advice, however, is to make the questions your own by using the language of your industry and the language of your buyers. I often find customers speak their own language. Salespeople talk in terms of features and benefits. The language of your customers is what people in their industry talk about in their meetings such as increasing revenue, decreasing costs, improving EBITDA, and increasing net income. So, we have to have discussions with our clients to understand the problem, understand the economic impact, and speak in the language of their customers. Salespeople who follow this process of proposing customized solutions in a way that matches the prospect's communication style have explosive sales growth, while those who use a shotgun approach typically do not see much growth at all in sales.

Once we've gone through this phase, we often work with salespeople to design messaging based on different personas, or the role they play within the organization. The easiest way to explain personas is through using an example I'm sure many of you can relate to. When I was living in Arizona, I needed to buy a vehicle. I wanted a big SUV to pull a fishing boat. Unfortunately for me, I brought my entire family to the car dealership with me. My wife wanted something like a minivan so she could drive the whole neighborhood to the mall. My son wanted a two-door sports car, and my daughter wanted something "cute." Each one of them is their own persona with their own needs and their own languages, so how the salesman proposed the solution made all the difference in what the outcome would be.

By the way, my wife won.

Usually, when I work in a B2B environment, some typical personas we work with are the C-suite: CEOs, CFOs, CTOs, and CROs. We might also work with a vice president of sales or human resources, quality and safety managers, plant managers, and engineers. All these people have their own language based on their own discipline. So, depending on who the influencers are in the sales opportunity you've just discovered, the onus is on you to adapt your messaging to those people, not only based on their role, but based on what you discovered about their personality, which we will discuss more in-depth in Chapter 3.

#6 Collaborate

"Coming together is a beginning, staying together is progress, and working together is success."
– Henry Ford

At this stage, we are seeking input from our prospective customers on the solution we proposed. This is another place where we put human-to-human sales into action. At this stage of the process, we want the customer to feel involved and not put on the spot to make a decision. When the buyer feels like their insight and experience were taken into account, they become an internal champion for the idea and will defend it to everyone else in their organization.

Without this collaborative stage, it is likely the prospect will only have a strong like or dislike for what is being offered based on any preconceived notions they gathered up to this point during the sales process. When they become part of the process, it helps them to better understand the problem they are trying to solve. It adds one more layer to the ideal solution, but more importantly, the decision maker feels their input is valued and they can then coach us on how to tailor our recommendation to be well received by the rest of their organization. This will, in turn, drive maximum impact.

It is much easier to move the proposal to a close when the decision makers help develop the recommended solutions. Throughout the sales process, we train salespeople to reinforce their value and ensure the customer does not have any objections. If we discover objections, we deal with them immediately. In our training, we recommend salespeople *handle* objections, not try to *overcome* them. We can't move to the next phase of the sales process until we have completely resolved the customer's objections.

#7 Negotiate

"The most difficult thing in any negotiation, almost, is making sure that you strip it of the emotion and deal with the facts."
– Howard Baker

Now, it's time to negotiate. If the prior steps are executed correctly, negotiation won't be that difficult. There shouldn't be many hard bargaining tactics because the prospect already feels like they have been working with you. In our negotiations workshop, we share the top 12 hard bargaining techniques and how to handle them. There are many strong thought leaders that teach negotiations, and Harvard has an excellent program teaching negotiation skills, if this is a skill your team would like to improve.

From my personal experience, I found 75% of buyers have received negotiation skills training, and, sadly, less than 20% of salespeople have received negotiation training. This skills mismatch often leaves money on the table you could have had trickle down to your bottom line. When I first started my sales career, I encountered many buyers in the grocery industry using hard bargaining negotiation strategies. However, when we engage with sales teams today, we identify the negotiation strategies they experience most and prepare them to professionally handle them while building relationships in the process.

One common negotiation tactic we see in B2B sales is called "split the difference." You have probably experienced this, but in case you have not, it sounds something like this. You proposed a solution for $50 that will perfectly solve the decision maker's problems, and they share that they can only spend $40. Then, they say something like, "Can you split the difference so we can get this product ordered? Let's settle on $45." In our workshops, we prepare salespeople to never split the difference but handle this tactic in a professional way that builds relationships and sets the tone for future negotiations. If this is an area you or your team are struggling with, I highly recommend reading the book *Never Split the Difference* by former FBI hostage negotiator Christopher Voss.

In some cases, if you have done all of the above steps, you may not need to negotiate at all, but it is a common step in most sales processes, which is why it's important to include.

#8 Close

"A sale is made on every call you make. Either you sell the client some stock or he sells you a reason he can't. Either way, a sale is made, the only question is who is gonna close?"
– Jim Young, *Boiler Room*

Once we finish negotiating, we move to the close, which is where we ask for the order. It's always astounding that 67% of salespeople never ask for the order. One of the most frustrating things as a CEO is to spend all that money on marketing, travel, and other expenses, only to find out your salesperson never asked for the order.
Why don't salespeople ask for the order?

That could be my next book, but the most common reason is they were never taught how. Without training in this skill, they are afraid. The fear of losing the sale or hurting the relationship with the customer is greater than their desire to achieve their goal of selling to the customer, serving them, and helping them solve their problems. So, they start their presentation and assume the customer will order when they are ready.

If a salesperson has a high need to be liked, they typically do not ask for the order. We perform a sales skills assessment to help us see each salesperson's level of mastery in closing skills. When I look at sales, my mindset is that I am helping people solve problems. Asking for the order is simply my way of wanting to get their agreement to work with me, so I can start helping them as soon as possible.

If you or someone on your team struggles with closing, I suggest you read James Muir's book *The Perfect Close*. I refer many of my clients to this book, and I am confident your team will improve your close rate after reading it. But in case you do not have the time or desire to pick up another book, I will quickly walk you through the two most common close techniques: the calendar close and the assumptive close.

When I helped a team that sold industrial air compressors, I coached them to use the calendar close method. This method uses concrete dates to create a sense of urgency for getting the order placed and delivered on time. In that industry, there is typically a 12-14-week lead time from the time you place the order to the time you receive it. A calendar close sounds something like this:

> "Frank, it sounds like a 70-horsepower variable speed compressor will best meet your needs, and based on the date of July 19th, we will need you to place that order by this Friday, so we can ensure the machine arrives on time."

The assumptive close is just what it sounds like. You are assuming the prospect wants to do business with you, and there are no objections to moving forward. It may sound something like this:

> "Barb, we appreciate you and your team helping us clearly understand the project, and it sounds like you agree your team would value business acumen training online to build a foundation in common financial terminology, value-based selling skills, and how to have conversations that lead to revenue. Let's start the program on May 12th."

If the close you attempted does not work, don't take it personally. Very rarely does the inability to close a sale mean you did something wrong. There is almost always an objection you have not yet discovered that is holding them back, and it is unlikely they will be forthcoming about what it is without you asking the right questions. This is why we need to get to the real issue, address it, and then try to close again.

#9 Revisit Impact

"The key to becoming relevant in the marketplace is to add value. The more value you can add the more relevant you will become."
–Germany Kent

Next, we should follow up on the impact made. This is something most salespeople fail to do, but part of the process is following up after you've delivered what you promised. What was the outcome? Did you deliver on what was promised? If the results delivered exceeded expectations, then it's time to ask that customer what else they might need help with.

Too many salespeople look at every customer opportunity as a one-and-done transaction, rather than a step toward building a lifelong relationship. Their goal should be to have lifetime customers, and the impact stage is instrumental in allowing the customer to look at what they've invested in and their return. Examine the journey together and understand the measurable results so far.

After implementing this simple sales process, one CEO shared, "Oh, we've been having more meetings with accounts than we've ever had in the history of our company. We have more quotes out than we've ever had before, and our close rate jumped 32%."

"Perfect. What else?" I asked him.

After doing win/loss research with the customers they recently won and quotes they lost, we discovered a recent quote they lost could have been won had the salesperson spent more time in the discovery and qualifying phase of the sales process. We quickly shared the real reasons why they did not win the quote with the CEO. The CEO called the customer to spend more time discovering the customer's needs and qualifying them. She received a $600,000 order at a 50% profit margin. That one sale delivered more than a 30X return on the investment for customer research.

If you want to have an unfair advantage over your competitors, always follow up on projects and share the results to understand the true impact.

Not only is it a great relationship builder, but, as we discussed, people buy based on the trust in and competence of the salesperson. In this step, you reinforce both. The best time to ask about other opportunities is soon after you brilliantly helped them solve a problem or fill a need.

Chapter 3: Assessment

"Change is only possible when an individual or members of a team have decided to change. In order to get it started, one must accept both the good and the bad of his or her current behavior."
– Robin Stuart Kotze

There has been more data created in the last three years than in all the years prior. Most people look at spreadsheets and try hard to identify patterns and actionable insights, but they don't have the time to do this well or the will to sit there and look at all of the data. With the technology we have available today, many data service partners are gifted at turning mountains of data into intelligent dashboards with actionable insights.

I was always taught prescription without diagnosis is malpractice. While the results of a shoddy prognosis in the business world may not result in physical death, it can absolutely lead to financial downfall. Business owners, especially those who are drowning in daily operations, are too often focused on quick fixes and bandages that will only stop the bleeding long enough for them to move on to the next biggest problem. They are wrapped up in treating the symptoms instead of the root causes, and understandably so. The symptoms are in your face and demanding attention, while the underlying causes require a lot of work to identify and treat. Let's face it, we are busy. Each day, there are dumpster fires that need to be put out, and we fall victim to the tyranny of urgency.

I was recently in the assessment step with a business owned by a young man, who had taken over for his father. The father was a true visionary, who had built a farming machines business from the ground up and turned it into a multi-million dollar enterprise. Now, the father is financially secure and enjoying his golden years, but the son doesn't understand why the business isn't growing as fast as when his dad ran it. Following my process, I asked question after question to this inexperienced entrepreneur who was quickly becoming agitated.

He looked directly at me and said, "Mark, I just want to grow. Why are you asking me all these damn questions?"

"Let me ask you another question," I said to him as politely as possible. "If you went to the doctor with shoulder pain, and his first solution was to cut you open and perform surgery, would you let him or walk away?" He was silent, so I continued. "You would probably want to have an MRI, some manipulation exercises, and maybe a second opinion. Am I right?"

After that, he got it. There are no quick fixes in business, even for me. Often, the biggest challenge for teams is to identify and discuss gaps. These gaps have been around for years, often from the inception of the business. However, they have grown to be the hush-hush problems we refuse to speak about. The first rule of Fight Club is "Don't talk about Fight Club." Many teams live under a similar understanding that it is not acceptable to talk about the gaps preventing success. I help teams face these gaps head-on, but this doesn't happen overnight, even with my framework. We need to work at it every day and remain consistent.

If you're thinking about whether or not any of this applies to your organization, I recommend taking an unbiased assessment of where you are at. This book can help you get where you want to go, but it is not here to decide on the direction for you. Start by asking yourself some of these questions:
- Who am I?
- What am I looking to create?
- How long do I want to be doing this?
- Where do I go from here?
- What is my desired outcome – grow it, sell it, go public?

The answers to these questions will provide the insight needed to begin the assessment of your business and make sure the strategy for growth is aligned with your vision.

When I conduct these various assessments, I am looking at a number of critical areas. Unlike the questions above, I focus on outward-facing questions that can sometimes be more painful to confront, which makes them that much more important.

- What problem does your product or service solve?
- Why do customers buy from you?
- Why don't customers buy from you?
- Who typically has this problem?
- How many people have this problem?
- Do they have the funds to solve this problem?

Then there is the big question most entrepreneurs who are enamored with their product or solution fail to ask....

Will they spend money to solve problems?

This is the first stumbling block in many, if not most, companies. There are many problems out there, and we have two basic choices: learn to live with them or solve them. If you decide to live with them, that's cool. Just prepare for the struggles that come with doing so. If you want to solve them, will you try to fix them in-house or spend the money to bring in a professional?

A key part of the process is intimately understanding our customers, their markets, the problems they face, and how they prefer to solve those problems. There are a lot of different areas we can assess, but it will not happen overnight. Business owners need to be receptive and trust the process. And most of the time, they are just too close to the trees to see the forest. That is where we come in to help them take a step back and look at all the angles.

When we work together, there are a lot of areas I look to assess, but the first thing I do is capture the voice of their customers, so we have an unbiased understanding of what is working and what isn't for the most important people in your organization – the ones who buy from you. Even as I write this, I'm torn between how basic it sounds and figuring out why so many business owners overlook such obvious areas of their operation. Trust me, if I can figure this out, anyone can. Remember, I was the kid the teachers wanted to put in the hall. So, let's unpack the assessment step in the *No Smoke and Mirrors* process and start identifying the gaps holding you back from success.

Voice of the Customer

"Punish your processes, not your people. Make sure customer complaints continue to be treated as a gift in your organization."
– Janelle Barlow & Klaus Moeller

When your team receives customer feedback, is it treated like a gift or a burden? Feedback, whether good or bad, is one of the best gifts your company can receive if you know how to act on it. The opportunity to improve relationships with your customers is when they are still willing to talk to you, not after they have already left. If a customer is willing to share negative feedback, it means they are at least willing to give you an opportunity to course correct. Too many business owners lose sight of the fact that their own opinions do not matter more than those of their customers. When I was a Managing Director at Pragmatic Marketing, a world-leading expert at training product managers and marketing leaders, the leaders there truly understood this principle, so much so that they gave their employees a coffee mug that said, "Your opinion, although interesting, is irrelevant."

The first thing we do when coming into a new company is ask for their list of customers by sales in descending order. This helps us understand who the top 20% of their customers are, and this is important because, more often than not, they represent 80% of their profit. We want to know how many total customers they have and how accurate their data is. We then break the book of business into four customer categories: A, B, C, & D, based on revenue and profit contribution, so we can decide on a statistically relevant number of people to call from each segment. The reason for this is that the questions are tailored specifically to each revenue tier.

Knowing our clients are already overwhelmed running their businesses, we design the survey and make the phone calls on their behalf. We have someone with a Ph.D. in marketing and customer research design the questions to gather actionable insights so that if any customers are trying to beat the survey by figuring out what the right answer is, they can't. We ask everybody the same questions, but the difference between us and most others is we are having phone calls with people and transcribing the calls instead of sending them a form or questionnaire. We capture the answer to every single question and comment they make. These comments by question become valuable when we design key account development strategies and plans.

If you are able to find the time and run this type of assessment for your customers, more power to you. I wrote a short ebook you can download for free off my website www.nosmokeandmirrors.com to help you conduct your own Voice of Customer research, or we can conduct the research and summarize it into an executive brief. Our team goes through the data, finds the trends and actionable insights, then creates 3-5 insight pillars to discuss. Together, we collaborate, discuss, and use our experience helping other businesses to create a plan to move the needle on your business.

Just to give you more context around how thorough this process can be, here is a sampling of the questions we will ask your customers:
- Why do they buy from you?
- Why don't they buy from you?
- What are they buying from other people they should be buying from you?
- Are they satisfied with the buying and service experience, and what can we do to improve this experience?
- What share of the customer's wallets do you have?
- What is your Net Promoter Score? (This is the survey many companies send out asking how likely you would be to refer friends and family)?
- Do different tiers of your business rate your business differently?
- How satisfied are your customers?
- What is their buying process today?
- What is their buying criteria?

- Who in their organization is typically involved in decision-making for products and services like yours?

In addition to asking these questions to the customers you are currently doing business with, we will also interview your ideal targeted customers, the ones you have always wanted to have a relationship with but have not been able to capitalize on. We interview your inactive clients in an effort to find out why their spending with you decreased or stopped altogether. It is important to identify why they replaced you and what you would have to do to win their business back. Too many times, I find companies are too quick to try and bring in new business while neglecting the opportunities to deepen existing and past relationships. In an ideal revenue mix, at least 85% of your growth target should come from existing customers with only 5%-10% coming from new clients.

If we ask salespeople (and we often do) what percent of the customer's wallet they think they have, they often proudly share the belief of having most, if not all. However, what we find when doing our research is most teams only have 25%-33% of the buyer's wallet, and there is a huge opportunity to grow revenue by winning your unfair share of the buyer's wallet while your competition fights for whatever is left.

I continue to be amazed by the information current and targeted prospects will share if you just ask the questions correctly. We have a process in which we start with very broad, rapport-building questions, then become much more specific. We ask the same questions to each person we call or meet with and distill their responses down into an executive brief. We gather so much information in this process it would take forever for a leadership team to review and act upon it, so we give them the trends and insights needed for account development plans.

A client of ours, who is a third-generation business owner, needed help with their post-COVID sales. Her company's business declined like most during the pandemic, but with the world getting back to normal, her revenue was still not growing. We asked for a list of customers by sales in descending order, and we needed to see the sales, contacts, and roles of each person involved with the accounts. We called a statistically significant number of their customers, and what we found was alarming to the leadership team. Their key accounts were in fact buying again at almost the same purchase levels as they had pre-pandemic, but not from my client.

The mid-tier revenue customers did not experience a sales decline during the pandemic. The lower-tier clients were actually up and running at pre-pandemic levels. It just did not make sense for the client to be experiencing such a difficult return to profitability. One of the first things we noticed was a big disconnect between what their salespeople input into their customer relationship management (CRM) system and what the customers were saying to our team. One of their top five accounts was preparing to defect – you know, drop them as a supplier.

Why were they about to get dropped? When our team hears something like a key customer is about to defect, they are instructed to dig as deep as the customer feels comfortable sharing. In this case, my client's current salesperson was not a good fit for this buyer. When we looked in the CRM, the salesperson made call notes such as:
- Customer is moving in a new direction, and we will see a significant drop in revenue.
- Customer is unhappy with the new price increase.
- Customer threatened to send their business elsewhere.

What the customer eventually shared was the new salesperson did not have much industry knowledge, and they felt like they were training them. The new salesperson did a poor job of communicating the recent much-needed price increase when he just emailed it and said it went into effect immediately. When the customer called the salesperson to challenge this, the customer was basically told to take it or leave it because this is what the CEO said to do. That's not necessarily the kind of conversation any salesperson should be having with a top-five account.

Could your salespeople be treating your customers this way? How would you know? When would you know, if ever?

This is when we jump right into action on our client's behalf. The time to save an account is before they leave, not once they are already out the door. Once they have left, it will take a great deal of effort, and often discounts, to win them back. So, my team gave me the transcript for the Voice of Customer interview, and I met with the CEO and VP of sales. I shared the feedback, and I was met with an overwhelming sense of disbelief. To the credit of the CEO and the VP, they called their client, met over lunch, and worked through the issues. Not only did they save the account, but they quoted projects currently being served by other vendors and grew their share of the wallet instead of just saving what was about to be lost.

Getting negative feedback from your customers can actually be a very good thing. As Janelle Barlow and Klaus Moeller tell us in their book *A Complaint is a Gift: Using Customer Feedback As a Strategic Tool:*

> Clients are always entitled to dissatisfaction, even if we consider their complaints absurd, unfounded or improper. By making a complaint, customers show that they still trust the company and offer it an opportunity to fix the situation. The least loyal clients don't spend their time on complaints. A fundamental change in attitude is required if businesses want to retain complaining customers. They need to learn to put themselves in the shoes of disappointed people's shoes and realize the value of a complaint for achieving their business goals.

I wish this was a very unusual case, a once-in-a-career conversation, but sadly, it is not. We hear this often – way too often. If you're reading this and thinking there is no way it can happen to you, humor me. Pick up the phone and call your top twenty accounts. Ask them some of the questions I mentioned earlier and see if you still believe your company is creating and capturing as much value and wallet share as you think you are.

I'll wait…

People

"The people process defines who is going to get it there."
– Michael Armstrong & Angela Baron

It's been said that people are our biggest asset, and I know this can absolutely be the truth in many circumstances. However, people can also be your biggest liability. There can be many reasons for this, such as hiring the wrong person for the wrong job, having ineffective job descriptions and poorly defined roles, or simply being a leader who does not invest the time or money into making sure your employees are being trained and coached for success. Even the most capable of people cannot fly if you clip their wings. Your responsibility to those on your team does not stop at hiring, it just begins there.

I have seen too many instances where leadership takes a hands-off approach to talent management, as they sit back and hope for the best. That is not fair to new employees, anyone in the company, or your shareholders for that matter. Take a second to think about this in your own organization. Who have you entrusted with training and coaching your teams?

I doubt you would expect your barber to give you medical advice or for your doctor to cut your hair. If that sounds ridiculous, then take a step back and ask yourself why you think the best salesperson in your company should also be in charge of training others.

Sure, it would be great to have them share best practices with their peers, but if they have no experience in designing modern training or mentoring others, then the skills will not translate properly. Roles evolve, people change, markets shift, and buyer requirements change, so how you navigate these nuances matters.

Please don't misunderstand – I'm not advocating a one-size-fits-all training approach or broad sweeping incentive plans to motivate people. Before you can even begin to help someone hone their skills, you need to know their current skills and where they need to go. Without understanding their personality type, communication style, and motivations for coming to work every day, you are likely to waste a ton of time and money on initiatives that appeal to only a small percentage of your team. That's why we spend a considerable amount of time assessing your talent in the same way we would our customers and financial reports.

As we assess our people, we leverage assessment instruments like DISC, as well as instruments for business competency. For example, with sales teams, we use a sales assessment that has over 90% predictive validity by OMG. We look at 21 sales skills, motivations, and beliefs. We produce a detailed team report by sales skill, as well as reports for each person to be used for individualized learning and coaching plans. This analysis scores each person on the sales team by role. In addition, you can see how your team compares to others in your industry and over 2 million other salespeople and sales leaders who have taken the assessment in the past. Our instrument also acts as a 360 assessment because we are looking at sales managers, sales VPs, and the teams that report to them.

We also have leadership team assessments. When I think about leadership, I always go back to what Ichak Adizes said in his book *Leading the Leaders: How to Enrich Your Style of Management and Handle People Whose Style Is Different From Yours,* "To be a leader means being able to lead. To know how to lead your subordinates, your colleagues, and even your boss, you must know how to handle all four styles."

Your leaders play a critical role in the success of your organization, but they can also unwittingly hinder progress. There is a concept referred to as the shadow of a leader, where the leader, who is skilled in a particular area and has specific beliefs, shares the same skills and beliefs as the rest of the team. This can be a good thing when the leader has the skills needed to be successful in their role and is aligned with the mission, vision, and values of the company, but it can also be a detriment when the leader is unqualified or unaligned. This is why it becomes critical

72

for each of your leaders to be aligned with the overall organizational goals, so their people are supporting those goals and not just pandering to what their immediate supervisor wants.

If we discover a leadership team is not aligned with the organizational goals, we use an instrument called The Five Behaviors assessment. This type of introspection can be more challenging than some of the others because it forces those in charge to take a look at where their gaps are and how their performance could be detrimental to the team. In Patrick Lencioni's book *The Five Dysfunctions of a Team,* he shares how elements like trust and the ability to have constructive conflict and debate are critical to the health of the organization. He also talks about how teams of leaders with diverse personality styles and skills can create a great deal of value if they have a foundation of trust.

So, we ask leadership teams to complete The Five Behaviors assessment to determine if this team can drive the results we are setting out to achieve or if we need to do some leadership training and coaching.

Scaling Up Assessment

"Don't try to control and improve all your thoughts, desires, and actions simultaneously. Make small steps towards your goal, set intermediate goals, and celebrate your achievements (especially when you are doing something you don't really enjoy)."
– Kelly McGonigal

When trying to improve the performance of your team, a good place to start is the Scaling Up Assessment, which is designed to help you understand four key disciplines of your company from a foundational level: people, strategy, cash, and execution. Focusing on those key areas will allow you to identify possible gaps preventing you from scaling your business to levels you never thought possible before. This isn't a grueling ordeal, like calling dozens of your customers for feedback. It only takes about five minutes per employee to complete, but it will uncover any weaknesses in the four critical areas. You can also run a report within seconds that will show you where the deepest shortfall is, so you can direct your attention accordingly. The free assessment can be found using the QR code on Page 161.

People

One of my favorite questions in the people section is, "If you had to start over today, would you hire everybody on your team again?" You would be shocked how many leaders say no without blinking an eye. There are other questions as well pertaining to having a repeatable sales process for employees to follow, which is another area where the answers tend to surprise us. Simply taking the time to identify and fix that area of opportunity will often lead to a 15% increase in sales on average.

Strategy

The next area is strategy. Out of all the questions in this part of the assessment, the ones I like to start reviewing with my clients are, "Do you have a business plan, and if so, is it a business plan that you developed with your management team?" Maybe you went to an off-site meeting and spent three days creating a business plan with your senior leadership team and a consultant or two. You may have left with a three-ring binder that's now collecting dust on your bookshelf, or it's a one-page document instrumental to the growth of your business. The plan should be discussed weekly and implemented daily because of just how fast business environments are changing on a regular basis.

Cash

When it comes to cash, most businesses fail because they run out of money, and one of the quickest ways to run out of money is by growing. Growth takes money. We use the Scaling Up Cash Flow Story Assessment, which involves sending them a spreadsheet to download their financial data. This allows us to model their cash flow and consider various scenarios for how they could be better utilizing that cash.

Do you have access to investment capital to help you grow? Is this something you need to self-fund? The Scaling Up methodology has a tool that can quickly assess your cash position today, and then guide you on what it needs to be in the future. It helps you experiment with different scenarios such as:

- What if we raised our prices?
- What if we collected our accounts receivables two days earlier or 20% cash upfront?
- What if we paid our vendors 3 days later?

After identifying the scenarios, we have thorough discussions about which strategies can get you there. There are all different strategies you can employ. I know one company that sold all the equipment in their plant to the bank, and then they leased it back, giving them millions of dollars of working capital. There are truly a lot of creative approaches if we find you have a shortfall of cash.

Execution

The last area is execution. Over 70% of changes fail because people don't execute, so we are going to really hammer that home here. I use the Scaling Up methodology planning software Scoreboard as a communication tool, which allows us to track execution daily, weekly, and quarterly. We identify what Stephen Covey refers to as your "big rocks," which are the things that significantly impact your business, then we track them to create a process that keeps the ball moving even in the face of a myriad of weekly interruptions.

There are a lot of brilliant plans out there that go unexecuted. Even though you may have several fires burning, you still have to execute. One of the biggest frustrations among most CEOs comes from spending 2-3 months developing a strategic plan, looking at their data and the market, gathering trends, maybe hiring a consultant like me, and spending around $15,000 a day, only to find no one is working on the plan six months into the year. This is a common problem because we get busy and default to old habits. Most plans involve some kind of behavior change. As human beings, we don't like change and tend to gravitate towards where we feel safe. Even when our safety net isn't working, it's what we've always done, so we fall back to the way we have always done things.

A lot of businesses are stuck in the "way we do things around here" mentality, but execution requires doing what works and taking new action. This is why a third-party perspective makes for a great coach. Just like if you want to improve your golf game, you'd hire a pro so they can tell you what changes you need to make and hold you accountable for sticking to those changes. When you drift back to your old habits, they will pull you back. But before we can think ahead to assessing progress, we need to evaluate how well your team executes today.

- Do they have the skills to execute?
- Do you have the structure to effectively execute?
- Do you have the tools, systems, and processes to consistently execute?

After going through this process with all of the company employees, we often ask the entire leadership team to take the next level of the Scaling Up Assessment, which gives us a much deeper dive into the business and the alignment among its leaders. This can be an incredibly powerful tool but is beyond the scope of this book. Once you have a handle on all the other action steps, we would be happy to get you started on the advanced techniques.

Once we have the results of the assessment, the CEO, business owner, and I then decide if we wish to engage. Is my team a good fit for the gaps we identified, and is this client a good fit for me? This is one of the hardest parts of my job because I have a huge desire to help everyone, but I need to eat my own dog food, so to speak, as I teach my clients in my qualifying skills and coaching course called Conversations That Lead to Revenue. I encourage my clients to use the same questions I use:

- Does the client have a problem we can solve?
- Is the problem urgent enough that they need to solve it?

- What is the economic and personal impact on my client once we solve it?
- Are they willing to invest time, resources, and finances to solve the problem?

Just as the client is determining if I'm a good fit for them, I am using my training and tools to quickly assess them and their personality to determine if I will deliver impact for this client and their team. If they want 5% growth over the next three years, I am not a good fit for them. I only work with clients who want to 2X, 3X, or even 10X their revenue.

DISC

"A management team requires people with different mindsets and management styles that can complement, rather than clone each other."
– Ichak Adizes

DISC is a very popular personality profile assessment because it looks at four different types of personalities, which becomes valuable in the process of helping companies grow and scale. This is where you find out if your people truly feel they can talk about things that matter, or if there are secrets everyone brushes under the rug. As Ichak Adizes says in his book *Leading the Leaders: How to Enrich Your Style of Management and Handle People Whose Style is Different from Yours,* "Misunderstandings are the main source of conflicts within an organization. If you want to be understood, you have to be the one who adapts." DISC helps us to understand our own personality style and the style of others, so we can adapt how we interact with others based on their style.

Before we go any further, let's take a look at what each personality type under the DISC method looks like:

- D: DOMINANCE – This style is both bold and skeptical. The D personality is a very focused problem solver, someone who dives head first into tasks and challenges. They are not always the most conversational and will speak in bullet points. Ds are often hungry for details but are not interested in taking the time to gather those details. It's better when someone else packages it, so they can just get right to work. As a D myself, I can tell you we are not very systematic. We want and need new challenges every day to stay engaged.

- I: INFLUENCE – This style is both bold and accepting. An I personality is very big on relationships and in-depth communication. You are not going to get away with speaking to an I in bullet points or assigning tasks with little direction. They need to feel immersed in the instructions and understand how the result will help to improve relationships.

- S: STEADINESS – This style is both cautious and accepting. An S tends to be the opposite of a D in that they need repeatability in order to feel secure. Showing up every day and working on the exact same task, similar to an assembly line worker, is where they are most comfortable.

- C: CONSCIENTIOUSNESS – This style is both cautious and skeptical. The C personality type wants data; the more you can provide them, the better. Before they can feel comfortable making a decision, they need to pore over reams of information. They don't like outright conflict but can be very passive-aggressive. So if there is a conflict, they won't bring it up again, but they will also likely never speak to you again either.

These traits are not the be-all and end-all of who a person is. In fact, many of us can have a combination of these personality types, though one trait is typically dominant. When one trait is more prominent than another, we refer to it as a "high" D, I, S, or C, and when it is less pronounced, they are rated as "low." While it is possible for someone to be a perfect balance of all four, it is extremely rare. Most of us will have one dominant trait with some elements of the others woven in, and we typically default to our dominant communication style. Think about a time when you had someone try to speak to you in a way you were not comfortable with.

Perhaps a high D leader was rattling off short, hasty directives to an employee, who identifies as a high I. Chances are, the employee will not hear or absorb a word the leader is saying because they require more substance. High Is are typically very interactive and thrive on building lasting relationships. If the same leader was speaking to a high S employee, they would likely feel similar toward the leader because they are very systematic. They find safety in processes, so it would be difficult for them to deviate at the whim of someone making abrupt changes. A high C, who has strong attention to detail and wants to avoid confrontation at all costs, might be better suited to handle the leadership style of a high D.

This all boils down to understanding who we are and who the other people are on our team and in our organization. It also highlights the need for diversity on a team if anything is going to be accomplished without constant personality conflicts. In order to help reinforce this, I like to put what we call a DISC wheel in the lunchroom. Everybody puts their personality style on the wheel, so no one has to remember where everyone falls. This is helpful when someone is running into a meeting with a teammate, and they know they should tailor their communication appropriately. If the person is a high D, you better have bullet points and be prepared for a brief meeting because that person is probably working on 30 things when they should only be doing 12. But if the meeting is with a high I, you should set aside 45 minutes, even if you (being a high D) only want to talk for 10.

The DISC assessment also helps ensure diversity within your organization. Too often, we get caught up thinking about diversity as a visible characteristic like sex, race, or disabilities. While those are all valid examples and are not to be diminished, there is also something to be said about the diversity within personalities and communication styles. If your entire organization is composed of high Ds, it would only be a matter of time before people start bumping heads and conflict arises. You will have a number of key objectives but lack the plans to execute them thoroughly. Similarly, if everyone was a high S, you may have analysis paralysis designing perfect repeatable systems, and chances are, nothing would ever get put into action.

This understanding of communication styles also impacts how well your people perform when they are talking with prospective customers. A sales team that is able to recognize personality types and adapt their communication style to mirror the person sitting across from them will have a competitive advantage over other sellers who are only trying to find ways to manipulate the conversation using outdated sales techniques. While that example refers specifically to the sales department, all areas of your business will benefit from your people improving how they interact with others internally and externally.

Sales Effectiveness and Improvement Analysis

"An efficient team consists of 8-10 people who have the same goal.
Horizontal ties within it are just as important as vertical ones."
– Robin Stuart-Kotze

If people are one of your constraints, then I would recommend we start by administering the Sales Effectiveness and Improvement Analysis (SEIA), which takes a holistic approach to analyze everyone on your sales team. There are 21 sales competencies in the assessment, and the final report will generally be in the area of 125 pages. The reports by individuals are ideal tools for creating individualized coaching and training methodologies. More importantly, it gives us insights into your team's strengths and weaknesses.

As an example, one area most teams struggle with is closing skills. 67% of salespeople never ask someone for a purchase order. That means they go through the entire sales process, explain your products and services, overcome objections, and simply wait for the prospect to actively make the purchase instead of trying any of the numerous ways one could try to close a deal. With the results from this assessment, we can tailor closing techniques to each individual personality on your team. The key takeaway is to meet people where they are and give them the tools, training, and coaching they need, instead of the ones we think they need.

One of my manufacturing CEOs came to me for help with his sales team. He shared how he desperately needed to raise prices due to inflation pressure on his gross margins and wanted to hire me for a two-day workshop on negotiation skills. He was very clear about what he felt his team needed, and the budget he planned was very generous. Much to his amazement, I declined. Instead, I suggested his team of 42 salespeople complete the Sales Effectiveness and Improvement Analysis from the Objective Management Group, so we could then prescribe training and coaching to ensure the price increase his team desperately needed to implement was well-received by their customers.

Within 10 days, we had the assessment results. The CEO and his sales leader were surprised to learn their team had very strong presentation skills, but very few of the other skills required to be successful in sales. They had a very high need to be liked by their clients and felt uncomfortable asking questions that could lead to additional revenue. This team was selling based on price, not the value they could provide to the client. They also lacked consultative selling skills, qualifying skills, and negotiation skills, to name a few.

We designed a training program to close the skills gaps, which included online training, virtual interactive training with application exercises, the live two-day workshop the CEO originally asked for, and new tools for the sales team to implement the much-needed price increases. The team did an excellent job of selling the price increase, negotiating, and collaborating with their accounts. In many instances, they improved their relationships based on trust and transparency. After 12 months, this CEO was running three shifts, gross margins were at targeted numbers, and his constraint moved from implementing a price increase and growing his revenue to hiring enough production workers to fill orders.

Internal Engagement Survey

"To win in the marketplace you must first win in the workplace."
– Doug Conant

Is the team engaged? Are they motivated? Are they aligned with the leader's vision? I can answer all those questions with data gathered from an internal engagement survey. This process is very similar to the Voice of the Customer, only it is geared towards your employees at all levels of the organization – because their opinions matter too. With internal engagement surveys, we meet with your leaders and the broader team. We want to find out how many of your people are engaged, how many are disengaged, and how many are just neutral or coasting by. The most recent data across all industries shows 50% of most teams fall into the last category of ambivalence, while a solid 18% are disengaged. Not only are employees not happy, but they are not even doing their jobs. That's a problem we need to solve sooner rather than later because it could negatively impact our business in ways we may not see on the surface.

Perceived Constraints

"Turning shortfalls into triumphs requires learning three disciplines: perception, action, and will."
– Ryan Holiday

There's a great book called *Theory of Constraints* by Eliyahu M. Goldratt that focuses on identifying roadblocks and openly talking about them. Goldratt asks the thought-provoking question about whether you will try to break through obstacles or bottlenecks when they arise or if you will continue to look for ways to circumvent the real issue. There are constantly new trainings, systems, and technologies available to us in the business world. Some companies catch on much quicker than others, with considerable rewards going to the early adopters. Just think about the advantage companies experienced over their competitors when they immediately embraced the internet rather than waiting a few years to get on board. If we don't factor in perceived constraints when building our strategy, they are likely to become real challenges at the worst possible time.

I ask business owners two questions when we get to this phase of the assessment: "What are we working with?" and "What are your perceived constraints?" From there, I meet and interview their team to see if they share the same perceived constraints as the leadership team. You would be shocked at how many times we immediately find a disconnect between what the people at the top think is the constraint and the feedback from those on the front lines. Typically, the person closest to the activity has more information than the leader who wrote the plan, and they are able to better articulate what is really stopping them from operating at a higher level.

Imagine you set the lofty goal of increasing daily shipments from 10 to 100. If the facility is open for twelve hours a day, you would need to make less than 10 shipments per hour. Sounds totally doable, right? Well, the warehouse supervisor might point out there is only one loading dock and the average time to stage and load a shipment is 30 minutes with his current team. The constraint of the existing setup will only allow for 20 shipments per day at best. Now, you have some choices to make. You can invest the money to knock down a few walls and add additional loading docks. If that isn't feasible, you could also consider extending business hours, adding an additional warehouse, or lowering the new shipping target. But without getting the feedback from everyone involved, you would never know what the true issues are and what the best solution would be.

One of the most challenging situations to identify perceived constraints in is with family-owned businesses that have been around for 20 years or more. The owners and senior managers have lived in the company and its culture seemingly forever, and they think they know the inner workings like the back of their hands. I can tell you the exact opposite is usually the case. They are so close to the trees that the termites are their focal point, not the forest around them. But when you bring in somebody from the outside, they can give you some fresh ideas.

I had a client who was struggling with growing revenue. The president asked me to work with sales, identify more new target accounts, and secure their business for their custom-machined products. They were convinced their constraint was selling and manpower to complete quotes and felt hopeless because they didn't have a plan or the means to hire additional workers. After digging a little deeper into their process, we discovered they had a bottleneck in their quoting process that needed to be fixed before we could increase the quote volume for new business. The turnaround time was averaging two weeks because they just didn't have enough people to handle the current volume – which could be a good problem in the right circumstances. It became clear that all the quotes were being processed manually, one at a time, which consumed tons of man-hours, and as the team tried to complete more quotes per hour, they started to experience errors that were costing the company profits on the sales they did win.

I introduced them to an AI-driven quoting configuration software that was capable of learning based on past entries. A prior client of mine used this in a custom tube bending business, and it significantly improved the speed and accuracy of their quotes. Each time they entered a new quote, the software became more intuitive and generated the quote faster than the one prior. It didn't require any human involvement other than gathering all the requirements to provide a quote and making sure the data inputs were accurate. Needless to say, they had no idea this technology existed, so they believed the only solution to their problem was hiring more engineers. This is only one of the hundreds of times I've encountered this when coming into a family-run business.

Once we all agreed on investing in new software to speed up the time to quote and significantly reduce the quote backlog, the results were staggering. Quotes went from taking almost two weeks to 24 hours in most cases. This wasn't just a huge relief in terms of relieving the bottleneck and freeing up people for other tasks, but it was a huge boost to revenue as well. Why? Most companies told us in our Voice of Customer interviews that when quotes are delivered within 24 hours, the buying decision is no longer about price. The response time helps them to take a task off their list and receive delivery sooner, which makes their business more efficient and, in turn, spurs them to give more business with the faster quoting company.

This one simple change in the quoting department resulted in the average closing rate increasing from 10% to 35%. That is additional revenue that came without having to increase any overhead. In fact, it reduced overall expenses because they were able to redeploy all of the personnel who were no longer needed to handle quotes. As customers received quotes within 24-48 hours, my client became a preferred vendor, the quote volume increased, and in some cases, their close rate actually grew to over 60% within 12 months. Acquiring this software was a one-time expense, but it had a payback equivalent to the salary of one and a half engineers. What started as a conversation to improve sales skills and identify new customers evolved into the elimination of a constraint this business had lived with for years.

Some common constraints can be:
- Capital
- Equipment
- The skills of your team
- Access to labor
- Supply issues
- Team structure
- Tools
- Systems
- Repeatable processes
- Leadership
- Marketing
- Warehouse or office space
- Digital assets
- SEO
- Buyer-centric sales plan

After finishing Voice of the Customer research for a very large trade association, where we interviewed 13,000 manufacturers, we expected our research to confirm the biggest constraints were access to labor and challenges with supply chain, but 80% of manufacturers said their biggest constraint was adding new business. Their teams didn't have the skills to reach out, contact, and engage with net new customers and open net new markets. They struggled to identify the ideal customers to be having conversations with to create potential new selling opportunities. That's a constraint!

Every year, new accounts come, and some grow, but accounts often leave. We must have a robust business development process to diversify our accounts so there isn't one client representing too large a percentage of total revenue. In this example, if you acknowledge your constraint to exist within your sales team, we would look at your sales skills assessment and dig deep into the particular skills they are lacking. Then, we would put a training or coaching plan in place to alleviate that constraint. We would conduct Voice of Customer research to understand your customer satisfaction levels and clearly understand why some clients stay and some leave.

If the constraint is not having salespeople, you can hire an independent sales team. Independent salespeople add a tremendous amount of value by leveraging their current relationships to help you win new accounts and grow your current ones. I am a big fan of hiring independent representatives. If this is new to you, they must be the right firms that call on the right buyers at the right time, and you must set clear role expectations and measure their performance. Independent reps sell multiple product lines to multiple accounts in their territory. They will introduce your product to their current buyers to gain more sales for your company.

If your constraint is sales skills and marketing skills, there are companies who can do the customer outreach for you while we build your internal sales and marketing competence. These companies can help you develop your ideal customer lists through market segments, leads to contact, and the messaging you should use. Years ago, these firms would basically "dial for dollars" with each call center associate making 50-150 calls per day trying to book future discussions. Today, these firms have added marketing services like digital asset development, messaging according to persona, and marketing sequences. They invest in technologies like Connect and Sell to call 250-300 contacts from your target list and have more conversations that lead to future discovery and qualifying meetings, which result in closing new business.

With all of these options, the only bad decision is to do nothing!

Transaction Data

"There are dollars in the data if you know where to look."
– Unknown

Ever since I realized just how valuable the information we already have access to can be, I tell all of my clients, "There are dollars in the data if you know where to look." But with more data harvested in the last three years than in all the prior years combined, it is getting harder to find relevant, actionable information. So, our team will spend time combing through your data and doing all kinds of slicing and dicing in search of trends we can gain insights from. When this information gets combined with the insights from your team's skills and what your customers are saying about you, just about all the pieces of the puzzle are out on the table for us to start putting them together.

Most business owners know data is important, but they lack the tools and methodologies to extract relevant insights. I always recommend systems like business intelligence dashboards to keep all of your metrics in one easy-to-find place. Once you know what information is most pertinent to your business, a strong IT person can implement a system like this for capturing and monitoring insightful data to help you take action.

At this stage of the evaluation process, we have no bias. We are simply trying to build a plan without trying to find data that supports our beliefs or desires. No matter the industry, we are going to look through transaction data as it pertains to invoices, pipeline value and health, product data, revenue by client, net profit by client, and so much more. We will look at the current figures and compare them against the same date from six months or a year earlier to see if there are any noticeable changes, both positive and negative. We will look through your CRM and answer questions about why you win some orders and lose others. Often, we call your customers and conduct win-loss analysis to find the answers we are looking for.

If you just read through the list of all the potential places you could start gathering data and feel like a deer in headlights, start with breaking down the percentage of revenue you derive from each of your clients after adding the cost of sale to your data. The graphic below is enlightening as it illustrates a fairly accurate representation of your three main customer segments. 20% of your customers are profit leakers, meaning they are costing you money every time you sell to them. 60% of your customers are breakeven, which means you hardly ever turn a substantial profit from their accounts. The final 20% of your customers generally create over 200% of your profit. They are the most important segment in your book of business and make up for the other poor-performing segments.

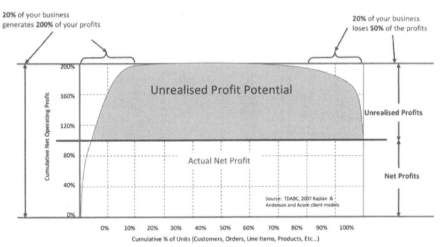

Image from Restaurant Technology Guys

So when we do our transaction data review, the first thing we're trying to do is find the profit leakers and fix them. We want to know who's contributing the most to your bottom line and find more new clients who look like them. Your most profitable clients likely have something in common, like their industry, revenue size, number of employees, region of the country, or other common traits.

In helping a client build a new website, I found a web developer who did great work and would have been a great fit for my client, but the client could not afford their fees. I offered the web developer my consulting services for free to help grow their business if he would do my client's site for a much lower fee. Though I don't usually do this, I saw it as an opportunity to help them both. The web developer agreed and got to work on my client's site while I dug into his transaction data.

Unbeknownst to the developer, six of his jobs in the last year were with hospitals, so I called the hospitals to find out what made them choose to work with this web company. I learned the sophistication of the security the developer used on the websites was particularly attractive to these hospitals. He never gave this a second thought in developing a business acquisition strategy, so we started targeting hospitals. Now, that's all his firm does.

He's up to a team of forty people now, who all focus on websites for hospitals. If it wasn't for the insight we gained from his transaction data and client interviews, it is unlikely he would have been able to experience such explosive growth so quickly. Thankfully, he did not fall victim to one of the pitfalls Goldsmith and Reiter mention in their book *What Got You Here Won't Get You There,* where "People who have already reached a certain level of success tend to take on bad habits, which prevent them from seeing possibilities and developing further."

Chapter 4: Desired Future State

"There are four pillars supporting grit: interest, practice, purpose, and hope."
– Angela Duckworth

The devil is in the details, and boy, have we just spent a lot of time up close and personal with the not-so-pleasant areas of your business. Now that we have identified your gaps, let's start looking at where you want to go. There is no perfect answer to this question, and it does not matter how long you have been in business, what size the company is, or what industry you operate in. You, as a business owner, need to set an honest benchmark for your business' desired future state and work diligently to plug any gaps that might stop you from getting there.

There have been so many books written about understanding the *why* behind what we do, so I won't subject you to any more reinforcement beyond saying I agree completely with clearly knowing where you want to go and the why behind it. In my line of work, I tend to get all kinds of answers to this question, but one was so profound I have to share it here to shine a light on just how important having a sense of purpose can be. Spoiler alert – it's not always about the money.

One young man in Europe had created an amazing software product he thought could be sold to a major company like Salesforce. He wanted to cash out on his labor of love for top dollar, but not because he had plans of buying a yacht or private airplane. His goal was to take all of the profits and use them to help others through his ministry work. Needless to say, this is not something I hear often. As a person with faith and belief in the need for ministry, I was sold on helping him with that mission – for free! Had he never shared with me the why, we might not have had the opportunity to work together.

In Angela Duckworth's book *Grit: The Power of Passion and Perseverance,* she says:

Having a clear hierarchy of goals will help you find your calling and will allow you to acquire and preserve your passion. Goals can be: 1) top-level (just one in every aspect of life), 2) medium-level (they serve to respond to the intermediary question of "why?"), or 3) low-level (tasks that, if completed, move you closer to attaining medium-level goals).

But having this clarity of goals alone will not get you very far. Once you know where you want to go, it is time to put together a road map for how you are going to get there. This is where capital can become a constraint. You want to grow but don't have access to cash, or you want to grow, but your building is too small. You want to grow, but you already have three shifts, and you can't imagine opening up another facility. How are you going to get there?

We start by meeting with everyone on your leadership team to collaborate and write your plan. We base our plan on data, not gut and intuition alone. We aren't just going to take an Excel spreadsheet of last year's sales and multiply it by a growth factor to get our new goal. That rarely works and is unlikely to be sustainable for 5 years or more.

InsideSales.com shared an interesting statistic that from 2016-2020, the number of sales reps achieving their goals has consistently declined. 2021 was the first year more people missed their goal than hit it, and I believe that is because we were more focused on math exercises than doing market research, working on the strategy, and planning to achieve the goals. I want my clients to show me their team has the skills to launch that new product, not just the financial projections. They need to be able to present the data showing the new product made sense based on the most recent sales trends and share the market research and the requirements their team gathered to design and launch this new product or service. But after asking for that information, all I usually hear are crickets in the boardroom and the copier in the hallway.

It feels like so much work when you're asked to do the market research upfront. I promise though, it's a much longer and painful process if you do the work later on. I call it "mullet marketing," like the old mullet haircut. It's short in the front, all business in the back. That's how most people launch a new product. They want to get it to market quickly. After all, it's such a smart idea they need to launch it before someone else does. The research usually ends up on the back burner, and before you realize it, you've spent millions of dollars launching a product that never hits sales projections or ROI targets. At the end of the day, the smart thing would have been to do the difficult work upfront.

Targets

"The great danger for most of us lies not in setting our aim too high and falling short; but in setting our aim too low, and achieving our mark."
– Michelangelo

When you shoot for the stars, you need to know which ones you are aiming at and have a plan for reaching them. Think of those stars as your key objectives, then formulate the plan. Our team helps clients develop specific account revenue growth plans by market, customer, product, and salesperson so they are aligned with achieving the key objectives. We'll build our plan from the customers, markets, and channels up as opposed to the way most businesses tend to do it from the top down. Account plans are usually designed something like:

> If you did $10 million last year, and you want to grow 5%, then you would take $10 million x 1.05. That becomes the goal for next year.

When we build our plan, the strategy might be to add more new products or gain a greater share of the high-value customer's business. We may assign a revenue number for a new product we are launching. We can also look at all the customers we have and assign them growth expectations based on how we expect revenues to grow. This is particularly critical when we build plans for your large key accounts.

There are a lot of different strategies we can use, but overall, we need to create a strategy for growing our key accounts and our business as a whole.

Let's say your team has an objective of hitting $50 million this year and your prior year sales were $40 million. You have worked with your sales team and created goals by account, particularly key accounts, and they total $45 million. How will you achieve $50 million? Well, you have options. Here are some of the common options we recommend, ranked in order:

- Raise prices: Far too many companies are selling products below what they could be. What impact would a 5% price increase have? Well, in our example, if your revenues last year were $40 million, a price increase of 5% would add an additional $2 million.
- Identify new clients in your current markets who fit the profile of your existing clients and sell to them.
- Review your transaction data: Determine if any revenue is coming from a new market, what market it is, what products they value based on purchases, and who in this market matches your ideal customer profile. Then, sell to them.
- Strategically acquire another company.
- Identify unmet market needs. Then, design and launch new products.
- Expand globally.

Working together with your team, we choose from the options above and assign revenue targets to each. If the goal is to achieve $50 million, your plan should have an opportunity of reaching $55 million or more because not all of your strategies will yield the desired outcome. Rarely is a growth plan a straight line. We start out, we learn, we adjust. and some of what we thought would happen doesn't happen or at least not in the timeframe we planned.

I'm going to provide you with solid content on what a good strategy looks like. I use the one-page business plan found in Scaling Up because I discovered over the years that people won't use anything more than one page. They likely won't read it, they won't understand it, and they won't know their role in achieving it. The one-page plan is crystal clear and helps you focus on the highest-priority items.

After we assign a revenue and profit goal to each customer, we also work with your salespeople and determine the behaviors we will need to execute to move our plan forward. What sales motions will deliver the greatest returns? That helps us go back full circle into forecasting net profit by customer analysis. The easy part is assigning a revenue goal to the customer based on the opportunity and what we know about them. Successfully reaching the profit objective for the customer is where it gets challenging.

We need to design the right terms of trade to help us achieve each customer's revenue and profit objective. We do that when we design our key account plans and our plans by market, customer, and employee. When we consider the plan for each account, we look at data like:
- Sales call frequency
- Mode of sales (face-to-face visits or virtual)
- Payment terms
- Other ways of delivering the product or service
- The turnaround time we will commit to

Once we've exhausted the growth we can achieve from our current business, we identify what we will need to acquire from new accounts. Let's say the business owner tells us, "Great news! We hit $10 million this year. Next year, we want to hit $12 million." Alright, so we've gone through the process I recommend. We identified the growth in each of his current customers and think they can achieve $11 million in revenue from them. Now, we need to go out and find a million dollars of net new business (net new logos as some teams call them), which is the number one concern of most manufacturers. We need to identify targeted accounts that match our ideal customer profile and create conversations that lead to revenue.

Structure

"Don't grasp for a silver bullet. In a time of crisis, there is not much to benefit from restructuring, new product launches, appointment of new charismatic leaders or capturing new markets."
– Jim Collins

For a long time, the structure for high-performing teams was thought of as a waterfall. We have an owner, and they have a series of VPs reporting to them. The VPs then have a series of managers reporting to them, and the managers have salespeople reporting to them. If it's manufacturing, they have several supervisors who have direct labor by workstation. Thus, the waterfall continues. But is that the best structure for you?

We decided to challenge that. One client was struggling with growth and declining gross profits. The structure in place was one they had used for over 40 years. After reviewing their growth goals, transaction data, and insights from Voice of Customer research, we determined they didn't need so many leadership roles high up in the organization. We found they were very top-heavy and lacked the resources in the actual customer-facing roles. There were too many chiefs asking for reports and not enough salespeople to do the research and still meet the needs of their customers. By designing a new and flatter structure with less oversight and more focus on the sales staff, we helped the CEO achieve their future revenue vision while improving the overall buying experience and customer satisfaction.

They now have two VPs reporting to the CEO instead of five, and each manager has no more than 8-12 direct reports. The structure change provided the funding to hire more customer-facing roles. Previously, their sales team was made up of 70% of team members in outside sales roles, and they traveled for face-to-face meetings with customers. Based on our Voice of Customer research, we also changed these customer-facing roles to a hybrid sales model, where 60%-70% of the structure is inside salespeople and only 30% of the sales team visits customers face to face.

Again, we use the internal assessment, transaction data, and the Voice of Customer research to design the ideal structure for your business based on what your customers want and need, as well as your desired future state.

Skills

"It's not about having the right opportunities. It's about handling the opportunities right."
– Mark Hunter

A big challenge a lot of companies face is designing a strategy but not having a team with the skills necessary to execute the new plan. When I was speaking at a conference to over 100 CEOs, senior leaders, and business owners, I asked them to raise their hands if they believe 100% of their people have the skills to execute the plans they have in place for growth. Not one hand went up, but that didn't surprise me because that's usually the case. Then I asked, "How about 70%? Does 70% of your team have the skills, tools, systems, and processes to succeed?" Still, no hands went up. I kept this process going until I was as low as 30% before the hands started going up.

Typically, what I hear from leaders is that 20% of their teams have it figured out. 20% don't actually want to be in a sales role, their current skill set is not in sales, and they would be more efficient in a different role. Around 60% are somewhere in between, just kind of trying to figure it out on their own. This is represented by the bell curve below.

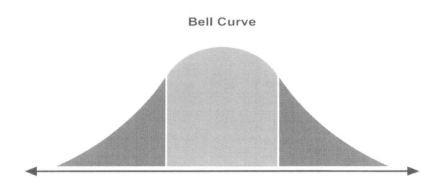

Through our different skill assessments, we are able to identify who the top 20% are and who the bottom 20% are. Then, we identify who is in the 60% of mid-level performers. If you really want to move the needle, imagine the impact on your bottom line if you can take the middle 60% of your team and have them improve their effectiveness and efficiency by just 5%-7% or even 10%. The trickle down to the bottom line is huge, but it can't be done if you don't have the data required to prepare a strategy for what you want to do and the skills required to do it.

My examples are often sales and marketing teams because this is the area I concentrate on most. However, we need to ensure we have the right people in the right roles with the right skills throughout the whole organization. Many of my clients value an exercise known as topgrading, which I borrowed from Bradford Smart's book called *Topgrading*. For this exercise, I ask the CEO to grade each member of their senior leadership team using the quadrant below. Then, we ask each of the senior leaders to grade their team members. We continue this process with each manager grading their teams. On the left axis is Core Vales from 0% - 100%, and the bottom is Productivity from 0% - 100%. This is how we identify our A and B players, as well as our C players.

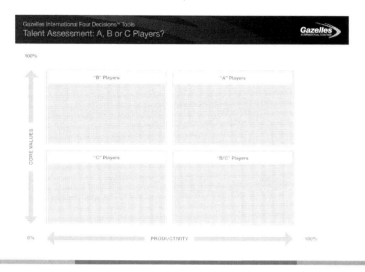

A players are high in core values and high in productivity. B players are high in core values but low in productivity. B/C players are low in core values but high in productivity. These are your most dangerous team members. Each team has them from my experience, and they are like a rotten apple that hurts a team's overall performance – another way of saying B/C is they are productive jerks. Then, there are those who have low productivity and low culture, who are C players.

Your C players will be those who were graded the lowest, and you can choose to train them up or coach them out of the organization. Managers tend to have strong opinions, often based on relationships, but I prefer to use the topgrading exercise to get an unbiased view of who can be coached up and who should be coached out. Often, we find team members identified as C players are in the wrong role or they lack the training and skills to do the role they are in. If we find this to be the case, we develop personalized learning plans for each C player to quickly upskill them to deliver more value in their roles, but only if the assessment instrument determines they are committed, have the desire, and, most importantly, are coachable.

Business Relationships

"If you take a sincere interest in others, they'll take a real interest in you. Build relationships, don't collect them."
– Rebekah Radice

Once we have account plans in place, I find this is a great opportunity to ask what new relationships need to be built with their current and new accounts. How can salespeople leverage the relationships they have with current customers to grow the business, and how many new relationships will they need to build with new accounts to achieve the growth objectives?

Ed Wallace, an author of multiple books on building relationships and one of my good friends, and I often provide workshops together to help teams improve their relationship skills. He shares how most business relationships are delivering less than 45% of their potential, and the most common reason for this is most salespeople have not been taught how to develop professional business relationships. In *Business Relationships That Last,* Ed shares techniques to help build better and stronger relationships with our current customers and our own teams.

Working with sales teams, we often find they need to strategically develop relationships with decision makers because they are not engaging with the actual decision makers during their sales process. Salespeople often have relationships with the buyers of the customer accounts they service. However, there are often many other people involved in the purchasing decisions of large organizations. Most purchase decisions are made by 4-6 people, so as we work on our account development plans, we develop a relationship matrix and train teams on how to build relationships with other decision makers. This training includes persona-based messaging, where we teach salespeople what business drivers are important to each person by role. For example, if quality managers influence a purchase, we will change our messaging and value conversations based on what is important to them.

High-performing salespeople build relationships to be viewed as trusted advisors, who are basically business consultants masquerading as salespeople. The days of being a sales rep are over, and they have been over for some time. If a decision maker wants information about a product or service, they can go on the internet and find it. What decision makers are hungry for are trusted advisors who share insights not available on websites. They want to have conversations with sales professionals who have the skills to ask questions to understand their customer's needs and make suggestions that will impact their customer's bottom line.

Building business relationships is one of the skills all top-performing salespeople have. We can teach salespeople how to build relationships with current decision makers and how to reach out to other leaders who influence purchases, but no one can teach salespeople how to authentically care about serving customers instead of just selling to them. It is more important than ever to have the right relationship-building people in sales roles because buyers can smell commission breath a mile away. By the nature of the questions asked, a good salesperson can demonstrate competence and build trust.

Explosive Growth

"Luck never built a business. Prosperity and growth come only to the business that systematically finds and exploits its potential."
– Peter Drucker

I recently met with someone who told me their current revenue was at $13 million, and they wanted it to be at $25 million in five years.

My quick reply was, "Would you like to be $25 million next year?"

He said, "Of course, but I've been told that's impossible."

So, I told him about the plastic fabrication company that went from $38 million to $79 million in one year. All we did was go out into the market, talk to the customers, and understand their problems. Then, we designed and launched products that completely solved their problems. I also shared the vehicle manufacturer with revenues stuck at $14 million for over five years before we interviewed their dealers and end users to search for unmet needs. That manufacturer grew to over $80 million within six years of applying the process. Nothing we are doing is all that fancy. We simply talk with people: dealers, distributors, end users, and influencers – human to human – to understand the challenges they face and suggest products and services to solve their problems completely.

Not everyone is looking for explosive growth in their business though. In my experience, it depends on who you're talking to. If you're talking to a VP of Sales in their late 50s just trying to comfortably glide into retirement, explosive growth may be too much work for them. Maybe they don't want to work that hard. If it's a CEO and owner, they may have created a lifestyle business they don't really want to invest in anymore because oftentimes, we need to invest as we start scaling. That investment could be in additional equipment, more people, purchasing and learning new sophisticated systems, or the cost of new capital sources to support and fund the growth. You are the owner of the business, and you set the pace at which you and your team are comfortable executing based on investments and effort.

If an owner with a nice lifestyle business is charging the company card to eat at 5-star restaurants every Friday night with their spouse, driving a Mercedes, and going on nice vacations, why would they want to complicate their life? I like to challenge these people because they're very vulnerable and eventually lose touch with their markets.

When we work with second and third-generation business owners, I let them know the model that has always worked for their grandparents or parents often does not work today. If they do not capture the voice of their customers, assess the skills of their teams, and invest in upskilling their people, processes, and systems, they will wake up one day wondering what happened because they aren't seeing the income they used to see. If they have not worked *on* their business for a long period of time, there is a good chance one day they won't even have enough money to make payroll.

Growing at least 10%-15% a year is manageable growth and won't disrupt your business. If you are not growing at least 15%, you're actually declining because of customer churn and rising costs. Every year, some accounts stay, and some leave. If you're not actively and methodically trying to grow your business, by default, you are declining.

I had three manufacturers who contacted me because their business had grown fairly successfully, but modestly, over the last few years. Then, all of a sudden, they woke up post-pandemic saying, "What happened?" Customers weren't calling and giving them orders. Their revenues went down 20%-30% or occasionally even more than that. They had a few key accounts defect because they lost touch with them and no longer understand what they want or need. They were working with outdated strategic plans, and they often felt they just needed to work harder and hold their people more accountable. They hit the point where they began to panic. They wanted me to bring things back to "normal," basically back to what the founder originally envisioned and accomplished.

It is natural for businesses that have been around for any significant length of time to lose sight of why they were started in the first place, especially when the original owners are no longer in the picture. They likely started the company because they saw a need in the market, and they had the means to address it. This obviously went well over the years for the business to still exist, but somewhere along the line, the consumers' needs changed. The same messaging and offering would no longer bring about the same result the owners were used to. Something had to change internally if there was to be any hope of once again meeting the external need that made them successful in the first place.

So, it was time to implement the *No Smoke and Mirrors process* and quickly reconnect to their market and buyers to understand their needs and how they are buying today. We conduct Voice of Customer research, perform team assessments, review transaction data, and build a customer-centric business plan. But again, not everyone wants to do all the heavy lifting. They may feel it's too much work, that it would cut into their personal lives, or they simply don't have the resources.

One of the responses I sometimes hear is, "I appreciate what you're saying, Mark, but I don't have a leadership team that can execute this."

Well, now is the best time to actually develop your leaders and bring new people on board. Train them and build the systems, or else you, as the owner, will be forced to be *in* your business so much, and you won't have any fun working *on* your business. But yes, there are folks who don't want to grow that fast. Maybe they are positioning themselves to sell their business, and they don't want to make those investments, but I would argue if they're positioning to sell, now is the time to make those investments and get a greater multiple at the time of sale. There are a lot of reasons why teams do not want to scale quickly, and we'll spend some time unpacking them to see if any resonate.

The other challenge I see more often is succession, where someone is being handed down their parent's business, but they don't want any part of it. In those cases, some people just decide to sell and hope they'll find the perfect buyer. Some people decide to find someone who will run the business and provide them with an equity position and salary. Others choose to sell the business to the current team.

If your plan for your business is a future liquidation event, you better make sure the business is profitable and worth something. Unfortunately, it comes as a shock to many business leaders when they hire somebody to help sell their business and learn it's worth much less than they expected because the valuation is based on a multiple of EBITDA, not an intangible number they had in their head. EBITDA, which stands for earnings before interest, taxes, depreciation, and amortization, is a measure of a company's baseline profitability for simply operating the business. The owner's knee-jerk reaction is to question how their years of blood, sweat, and tears in this company don't hold the value they thought. Smart future owners are going to pay a multiple of the EBITDA and consider the strategic impact acquiring your business will have in their strategic growth plans.

You can always sell assets, anything from real estate and equipment to intellectual property – but getting any significant value from the business itself will be a longshot if it is dependant entirely on the owner's involvement.

Chapter 5: Identifying & Closing Gaps

"When you face an obstacle, practice objectivity, control your emotions and focus on what can be done. Try to realize that no crisis will last forever, and any error you make is just a blip on the map."
– Ryan Holiday

With all of your assessments complete and transaction data thoroughly digested, it is time to see what is working well and what requires improvement. The areas performing well are the easy part of the equation. You might find minor improvements that can be made to enhance the results, but otherwise, don't break what is already working. Identifying the gaps isn't rocket science, but the struggle often lies in the business owner not wanting to admit there is a real issue. That's why we base all of the findings on research. Numbers don't lie. Sure, you can try to twist them in your favor, but at the end of the day, the answers will be right in front of your face.

With the gaps out in the open and everyone in agreement that something must be done, we have to prioritize which gaps we are going to address first. Most companies will not have the resources or manpower to work on everything at once (although most will want to), and even if they could, the disruption caused to the organization would do more harm than good. The gaps we are concerned with the most are the ones with the greatest impact on achieving your future vision, including which ones stand to lose you the most money if not addressed right away or which ones can result in the most significant revenue gain if addressed immediately. We might be able to pick the top two or three, depending on how extensive they are, but not more than that. We can always come back to the other gaps after we've successfully closed the ones we are working on.

I was approached by a fourth-generation family business owner who was struggling with revenue growth. As you might have guessed by now, it all starts with the data because numbers don't lie, but we do have to dig a little deeper to get a clear picture of what is going on. I followed the process and began by interviewing all of their leaders, managers, top accounts, accounts who left, and some of the largest new prospects (whales) they were targeting. We analyzed their transaction data, assessed the skills of their team, and performed a digital footprint audit on their website. With all of that information in hand, I sat down with the executive team to present the findings, but they didn't believe the data.

In my line of work, I find there are two types of executives: those who are focused on gathering data and making smart, strategic decisions to profitably grow their companies, and those who just hire you to validate what they believe to already be true. This was the latter type of situation. They didn't want to hear the data or insights to scale their company. The family members wanted me to deliver a report they could bring to the executive team and say, "I told you so."

Sorry, but that's not the way I operate. I basically had to tell them their baby was ugly. This was a family-owned business, and one of the grandsons was preparing to take over. I had no intention of telling them what they wanted to hear. Instead, I shared insights with him no one else ever brought up before. My conversation went something like this:

> Your assumption that you're the only one in the country who offers this product is wrong. I found three other competitors that make it. Your assumption that your customers really value this (———) is incorrect – they don't. They valued this once, but today, it takes table stakes to be in the game. The assumption that your pricing is market-based, based on value, is not correct. Your price is double your competitors' prices, and your key accounts shared that knowing this makes them wonder if they are paying too much for what they buy from you. Your turnaround time on quotes is two weeks longer than your competitors, and your issue with shipping on time is a real problem for your clients buying just in time.

It was clear they did not want to listen to anything I had to say, and I had to remind myself of why I was even there to begin with. In the last 18 months, their revenue had dropped over 38%, and a friend of mine referred them to me and suggested my *No Smoke and Mirrors* process. We met, I shared the model, and they loved it. Their CEO was thrilled to finally find someone who would build a growth strategy based on data. His flawed assumption, however, was that we would find data to support his and his senior leadership teams' dated beliefs.

The downfall of this company will eventually be the combination of their inability to adapt and their hubris. The first is manageable since not every business needs to grow exponentially to survive, but hubris is always deadly. Because of this mentality, I tell prospective clients upfront they should not hire me if they are looking for someone to agree with everything they currently do. I'm not that guy. Just like your doctor won't lie about a health condition, I won't pretend your business isn't broken if we find gaps preventing your profitable growth.

We are going to revisit some of the assessments from Chapter 3, so we can see how they are applicable in identifying the gaps holding us back from getting to where we want to go. You only have so much time in the day, so it is important to figure out where the most damage is being done or where the most impact can be made, then focus your efforts on starting there. Once you have a handle on where the greatest threats and opportunity gaps are, we can make a plan for closing them.

From my experience, the most impactful gaps tend to fall into one of the 9 steps in the sales process we looked at in Chapter 2. That's not to say they are the end-all and be-all or closing them will immediately solve all your problems, but they are the ones that will kill you the quickest. As we go through these areas, reflect back on your own business and honestly think about how many of them might be at play right this very minute and what steps you can take to work on them going forward.

Understanding

"Seek first to understand, then be understood."
– Stephen Covey

When we speak about understanding, it applies to both customers and the marketplace in which a business operates. So many owners have an ingrained belief – a bias almost – of how much they truly know about their customers. The relationship has been around for so long that they believe they know how their customers work, what their customers value, and what their customers don't value. In reality, businesses change all the time and more significantly than ever since COVID. We now find that understanding is the most pervasive of the five gaps. Businesses no longer understand their customers as intimately as they did when they first opened their doors.

For example, one of my clients supplies very large automotive companies. For years, they have grown based on their reputation for quality and shipping truckloads of parts on time. Post-pandemic, a number of their key customers did not reengage and never started ordering truckloads again. Being that we serve other clients who provide parts to the automotive market and saw their sales increase, we were confused why this client's sales were not growing at the same pace as other clients. We conducted Voice of Customer research by contacting their top 50 accounts and heard one common thread, "When our requirements are up to truckload quantities again, we will place orders from you, but today, we are operating 'just in time' until we know what the new normal will be." My client quickly changed their messaging and reduced their minimum order requirements. Sales grew over 200% within 60 days. The sales continued to grow with current customers, and they started winning new customers as well. Sales grew so much that they had to start a third shift to meet demand.

Why?

We learned the buyers had changed their requirements and adjusted to what we understood customers valued today.

When was the last time you interviewed, not tried to sell to, your top 20-50 customers to make sure you clearly understood their current needs, buying criteria, and challenges? You can find a list of helpful questions we use to interview customers to ensure understanding by using the QR code on Page 161.

Sales Process

"A sales process is a systematic, multistep approach that enables a sales force to close more deals and increase margins. An effective sales process is built back from a customer buying journey."
– Gartner

Most teams believe they have a formalized, repeatable sales process, when in reality, they don't. The business owner swears they do, but when we assess the sales team, no one knows what it is, or there is a formal sales process in their CRM, but few on the team are following it, resulting in lost business you could have and should have won. So, what we have here is a two-pronged issue: creating a sales process and ensuring our teams are following it.

Let's start with the first issue. How do we create a formal sales process that strategically delivers the results your team wants and needs? Here is the sequential framework we use:
1. Ideal customer profile
2. Rapport
3. Discovery
4. Qualify
5. Propose solutions
6. Collaborate
7. Negotiate
8. Close

9. Revisit Impact

This process has delivered the best results consistently over the past 30+ years, and we have already discussed the proper way to execute this in Chapter 2. The framework is always the same, but what we use in each step is customized to your sales culture, market, products, and decision-maker personas. Despite the simplicity and predictability of the steps, this still remains one of the biggest areas where we identify gaps. When we isolate each of these stages, it is easier to figure out which stage the gaps live in so we can then figure out how to close them. Teams that implement a formally defined sales process and are trained on how to use them typically realize a 15% increase in sales in the next 12 months.

While a 15% per year increase in sales sounds nice, considering how to make such a drastic increase in sales is an interruption to the normal everyday process for a lot of businesses. When I work, particularly with manufacturers, they are looking for slow growth of 3%, 5%, or 6%, but they don't take the market's growth into consideration. If you plan to do a price increase, you can raise the cost of your product by 3% to meet your goal without any additional effort from the sales team to add new business. Now, think about your costs. I'm not an accountant, but I've worked with some amazing accountants who taught me that if we're not growing at least 12%-15% a year, we're not even keeping up with our costs.

So, if your business doesn't have a plan to grow your sales 12%-15% at a minimum, then you're actually declining, which you will see by the end of the year. This is why sales plays a key role in business. While we could spend the majority of this chapter discussing how your sales team can prevent your business from going under, I'd rather help you find, understand, and fix the gaps in your sales team. The most challenging part of the sale, which our research has shown, is knowing how to have a conversation with another person, discover their problems, understand what they're willing to pay to solve those problems, and then solve those problems brilliantly. If you think you have major gaps in your sales process, I encourage you to go back and reread Chapter 2.

Leadership

"Rebuilding a company requires staying loyal to corporate principles and values, getting back to solid management disciplines, using rational management methods and the belief that the company will be able to become great and thrive again."
– Jim Collins

If we identify one of the gaps preventing your growth as leadership, there are a number of instruments we can use to get to the root cause. Some of the most common reasons we find gaps in leadership are a lack of trust among the leadership team, the inability to have constructive conversations, and poor execution. We often find a lack of training, motivation, and alignment to be issues as well. The problem with a gap in leadership is the leader often does not want to admit or does not believe they or one of their trusted leaders could be part of the problem, but if you bury your head in the sand, it will only get worse. Once discovered, it can be improved with training and coaching – if the person is coachable, that is.

Think about this question as it relates to yourself and your organization. How many of your senior leaders, including you, have been trained to be leaders? If you are like many of the teams I work with, the answer is probably very few. If you are a newer or smaller company, this issue might not surface early on since many of your leaders are serving in the capacity of player-coaches, rolling up their sleeves and getting work done right alongside the teams they lead. But as you scale and grow, the leader's role must evolve into one that focuses more on leading and less on doing.

The Peter principle is a management concept where you promote somebody to their level of inefficiency. If we find someone on the leadership team does not have the skills or the desire to be coached, we typically try to find another role in the organization where they can add a tremendous amount of value. Then, we bring someone in who can lead that particular segment of the business.

When gaps in leadership go unaddressed, they create a ripple effect and magnify the negative reach of the shadow of a leader we mentioned earlier. It is not unusual for everyone reporting to the leader to share similar motivations and beliefs, so this can get dangerous quickly. The problem compounds as you grow and scale, because now you have new people joining the organization who fall into this false belief and become unsure of what is real and what is just accepted norms. Bad habits begin to snowball quickly.

That is why we engage and assess your leadership team – we are looking for the level of trust, accountability, alignment, and ability to have critical conversations, as well as if each leader has the skilled required for a future in their role. We really need to make sure your leadership team is aligned and firing on all cylinders. We like to make sure everybody on your team understands the objectives for the coming year, the next three years, and often, what we refer to as your BHAG, which might be five to ten years from now.

Next, we determine if everyone on the leadership team is aligned with the growth strategy. Often, we meet with leadership teams of 5-8 people, and it's not unusual to find at least two people who aren't completely on board. It is critical to find those people early and identify why they're not, then either help them get on board, find a different role, or exit the company so you can find new talent to add to the leadership team. From my experience, 90% of the time, we can get leaders who are not aligned back on board with additional training and coaching. However, if we find someone on the leadership team who is not aligned and is undermining the CEO's vision, they have to go and go quickly. Each leader on your team casts a shadow over the team they lead, and we must ensure they are aligned with the vision.

One particular client we worked with had a really robust strategy they spent a lot of time developing. It looked like they crossed all their Ts and dotted all their Is, but six months in, they found performance was still lacking. In these cases, we typically track this back to the root, which is what we did. It turned out the leader in charge of that area wasn't fully on board. As we interviewed the team members, we discovered they were instructed to disregard the strategy because their leader did not feel it made sense. This is why assessment instruments are useful. Leaders will often all be on board and say the right things in management meetings, but water cooler conversations and individual team meetings tell a different story. Assessment instruments and team-building exercises help us quickly find those leaders.

Ultimately, it boils down to whether or not you trust your other leaders and if you believe in your company's vision. You're not going to get top performance out of your team until you've built that foundation of trust. Usually, when a leader is not on board, they don't clearly understand the vision or don't trust the plan. It's no surprise when that person's direct reports aren't performing at their best either then. It becomes evident when people are going through the motions and lack that fire in their gut to get it done. They also are not overcoming obstacles; instead, they're subconsciously looking for obstacles that validate their belief and their leader's belief that what they're doing doesn't make sense.

Some other key areas to be concerned with when it comes to leadership shortcomings would be:
- Having the right person in the right role.
- Having the right skills for the right role.
- Ensuring all of your people are coachable.
- Creating an environment of trust.

I cannot underestimate how important that last bullet point is. If you haven't had a chance to read Stephen Covey's book *The Speed of Trust*, I highly recommend you do. My big takeaway was that most businesses have a trust tax against their profits that never shows up anywhere on their financial reports. This isn't a tax in the physical sense of the word, but more of a phantom cost that erodes the bottom line when teams don't trust each other or their leader. They're doing a lot of unnecessary and often redundant activities instead of talking about things that really matter, and efficiency is negatively impacted in the process. An inefficient company will struggle to survive, let alone scale.

One way we build trust is by leveraging the DISC assessment, which helps us understand what your personality style is, how you like to communicate, and, more importantly, how you like others to communicate with you. Upon identifying each of the leaders' top personality styles, we plot them on a personality wheel and coach leaders on how to have meetings with other leaders on the team. We want leadership teams that are diverse across many areas such as personality, race, sex, religion, and diversity of thought (my personal favorite) to ensure no one falls victim to a groupthink mentality. Studies show diverse leadership teams have the highest profitability margin. You don't want every leader on your team to be in the high D category. If everyone's too focused on execution, no one will take the time to create a plan and implement systems and processes. Once we develop an understanding of each person's style, we also develop a process and teach them how to adapt their conversation based on the person that they're meeting with.

Team

"Innovation is the lifeblood of an organization. Knowing how to lead and work with creative people requires knowledge and action that often goes against the typical organizational structure. Protect unusual people from bureaucracy and legalism typical of organizations."
– Max De Pree

The sad truth is most people structure their teams wrong. I see it happen all the time. A company will over-leverage the skills of an employee who may be great at a particular duty within a department and make them a manager, department head, or leader but fail to provide leadership skills training. The once rockstar employee then crashes and burns. Not everything fits neatly into a box, and, as leaders, we need to recognize that by looking beyond specific skill sets. It often takes a catastrophic event, like a global pandemic, before gaps within our teams are either recognized or addressed. By that time, it is too late – the damage is too great.

If we are going to take the initiative and make those changes sooner rather than later, we first have to identify roles. Once the role is identified, we can hone in on what skills will be required and have open discussions with all stakeholders about those requirements, so we can work on closing the gaps. If we have an employee who is a great writer, we can identify early on that they lacked the SEO experience required to be the head of marketing. Then, as a group, we could decide just how important that skill set is for the person heading our marketing team to have. It may sound obvious for the head of marketing to be versed in SEO, but the reality is too many promotion decisions are made because a person excels at one thing, and the rest of their gaps are ignored. We often find people in leadership roles based on their years of service and pay grade. not their skills and ability to lead.

Using this approach, you can avoid the trap of trying to figure out how to take care of the legacy people in your organization, who might not have the right skills to remain in their current positions. The best thing you can do is put them in a place where they can thrive based on their current skills and training. To do otherwise would be a disservice to the legacy employees and the company. Once they know they are not qualified to take on the new role you assigned them, they will panic, their performance will suffer, and profitability will be negatively impacted.

In fact, one of the assessment instruments I use for salespeople consistently shows about 20% of your sales team should not even be in sales. So, if you're frustrated with how things are playing out in your organization, use the techniques in this section to evaluate who you have where and why. The assessment instrument will tell you if they're committed, if they have the desire to succeed, if they're motivated, and if they're coachable. It will quickly become apparent if they just don't have the skills and or the will to sell. Once you have assessed all the gaps, you become aware of the skills your people have. That knowledge can help you ensure they are in the right roles and set up for success.

Businesses usually create an organizational structure where a subject matter expert is responsible for their specific department. For example, the marketing expert runs sales and marketing, then the top salesperson leads sales, etc. I'm here to challenge that structure. When I work with my clients, I use an empty boxes exercise to help them identify the roles they need to fill within their organization. The only thing you need to get started on this exercise is a pack of sticky notes and a flat surface.

Do not put names on the sticky notes just yet. Instead, on the sticky notes, write down roles and what skills a top performer in that role would need to be successful, how that role will be measured, and what KPIs will be monitored. Then, write down who on your team can fill that role. It is not unusual to have a role and no one on your team with the right skills, beliefs, and motivations to fill it. If we find this to be the case, we explore bringing in new employees to fill role gaps. The role exercise will help you customize your pre-hire assessment instrument to identify candidates most likely to succeed in this role.

At the end of this exercise, it's not uncommon to have team members whose names are not on a sticky note because they do not fit the new team structure. A person may be loyal and committed to the company, but their skills do not match any of the roles. If we determine they are coachable, committed, and have the desire to grow, we can train and coach them in the ways we will discuss in the upcoming sections. If they are a C player, who has never excelled in a role and is not coachable, we need to coach them out of the organization. This is the hard part of leading teams, particularly those that are scaling. The talent that got you to this point often lacks the skills to get you to the next level. We always first try to coach, train, and upskill them to meet the requirements of their role based on today's environment; however, if they are not willing to be trained or coached, they need to exit for the sake of the team.

Coaching

"Use external help to develop grit outside-in. Parents, teachers, trainers, coaches, bosses, and friends are there to support you in a time of need and help you to soldier on when you're ready to throw in the towel."
– Angela Duckworth

People with a fixed mindset believe abilities are innate and stay the same during their lifetime. Every situation calls for a confirmation of their intelligence, personality, or character. They strive for control and excellence; otherwise, they lose interest. People with a growth mindset believe what they are dealt with is just the starting point for development, and their best qualities can be cultivated through effort, strategies, and help from others. They love taking risks and confronting challenges. The same principle holds true for business. No matter how good you are at your profession, the presence of a coach will help you to continue performing at the highest level and reach new plateaus you never dreamed possible.

One of the reasons my clients get such great results is that they come prepared for our coaching sessions. We create and send them an agenda ahead of our sessions and encourage them to share anything they are struggling with. We use a coaching model based on the Foursquare Coaching Framework to make our sessions quicker, easier, and more fulfilling. Our discussions are focused on action steps and their corresponding results, as well as if they align with achieving our key objectives and overall goals. When it comes to sales, I have yet to meet a salesperson who is not busy and feels they have enough hours in the day to accomplish their goals. However, we have to determine if their activities align with their key objectives.

I read one study that, on average, salespeople spend less than 20% of their "sellable time" actually selling. If that's true, what are they doing? They are filling their days with administrative tasks, building reports for their leaders, entering information in their CRM, researching account lists to determine the best prospects to call, and helping other areas of the business like quality assurance and accounts receivables. If they are an outside salesperson, there is time spent traveling, booking rental cars and hotels, and creating expense reports.

Salespeople are always busy, but we often find we need to coach them and guide them back to activities that support goal achievement. Typically, when we have coaching conversations with salespeople, we ask them to share their activity and results, then we ask questions to help them bust through areas where they may be stuck. If a salesperson were to tell us they are struggling to make contact with buyers to close a sale because their buyers are incredibly busy, I would ask open-ended questions such as:

- How would you like somebody to get in contact with you if you were busy with other obligations?
- Who do you know that knows the buyer you are trying to contact? Can any of these people connect you with the buyer?
- What methods of contact haven't you tried yet?
- Who on your team has had experience reaching out to buyers who are difficult to get in touch with? What was successful for them in those situations?

Good coaching helps the employee solve the problem, while micromanagement requires employees to come back to you every time they have a problem. A manager gives you the solution to a problem, but a coach will help you find a solution on your own. What's currently happening in the job market, particularly with Millennials and Gen Zs, is they don't want to be managed, so managers are struggling to manage them. This is why I encourage leaders to be a coach instead of a manager, and it's been life-changing for businesses.

Coaching is a process, and a good coach won't have all the answers – I guess that makes me a great coach! My recommendation is to have clear expectations for each coaching call so the associate comes prepared, and you have amazing questions ready. But make sure you coach by letting your associate answer the questions themselves. Admittedly, I've gone about this the wrong way in the past. I used to think my role as a coach was to listen and tell people what to do. The problem is that leaves them with no ownership, and they are destined to repeat behaviors that do not drive desired results.

The approach I recommend when coaching people, whether they're salespeople or someone in a non-selling role, is to have them share a vision of where they'd like to go. Then, share what skills are required for them to meet those goals. Again, we have to follow the process where the team member is aware of the meeting's agenda ahead of time. We recommend you follow the Foursquare model, and let the other person bring their issues to light in the places they're stuck. Collaborate with them to help them get to the answer themselves. The next time you get together, it will be an entirely different conversation, where the other person is doing all the talking. Your job is to coach them. You might share your experience and training, and use your experience in the business, in the market, and in the channel to coach them in directions to help them succeed.

Chapter 6: Effective Training Methodologies

"All organizations have identical systems consisting of work, connections and routes. Industry leaders, or the "rabbits" leading the pack, have a different approach to managing complex operations."
– Steven Spear

The problem with outdated sales training methodologies is the constant need to refresh and review them. Studies show within 48 hours of learning something new, we forget it unless we have some sort of reinforcement. This is called Ebbinghaus's Forgetting Curve. So, when someone approaches us and asks us to do a training, we make sure to let them know training is not a one-and-done event.

There is a lot of really bad training out there. The global corporate training industry is an over $75 billion business and growing rapidly at anywhere from 20%-30% per year. Ironically, the reason it's growing is because many training companies are not actually making a difference. None of the material is sticking with the participants, and they wind up having to take it again, often from a different provider, because the participants forget 90% of what they were taught and slip back into their old routines within 48 hours of finishing the course.

The sales training industry accounts for about $2 billion and is expected to grow around 14% each year for the next five years. Because 50% of all salespeople have never been trained, a lot of new companies are offering a variety of options to get them up and running as quickly as possible. Those courses cost your company anywhere from $6,000-$9,000 per person, and at the end, they have them kneel down to get tapped on both shoulders with a sword. Congratulations! They're now sales warriors, right? No – not if you were paying attention to any of the statistics we just went through.

Ultimately, the process used to find skills gaps is broken, so current training models are designed to throw the whole kitchen sink at everybody rather than give people what they need in the areas they need it. When a trainee gets to a section of training they don't need, it drastically hurts engagement, and they might mentally check out or physically sign out of the whole program after the first class and miss something they desperately needed. As a business leader, you need to challenge training companies to give you what you need, rather than just a one-size-fits-all program they designed a few years ago.

In my career, I have experienced two types of training objectives in businesses. One is the "check the box" kind. In other words, someone on the senior leadership team said to find and deliver training. So, you find it, deliver it, and check the box – done. Unfortunately, training has been looked at as "checking a box" for many years. Once a need has been identified, it's easy to bring in a trainer and have a training session complete in just a day and a half. However, that's not effective training because it leaves employees victim to Ebbinghaus's Forgetting Curve. If someone wants to provide training and coaching simply to check a box, we do not engage. The training and coaching we deliver are designed to deliver an impact, not check a box.

The second approach is where someone in senior leadership identifies a particular goal not being met on a consistent basis. In these cases, most good leaders try to find the source of the goal not being met by performing observations of employees in relevant departments. There are many methods of observation including ride-alongs, shadowing, or four-legged sales calls. When they do this, they aren't just looking for the team member falling short, they are also looking for team members who are exceeding expectations in these roles. Then, they compare the star employee to others and seek training to improve the performance of the overall team.

Back in the day, before we had all these assessment instruments, all we could do to understand what the best salesperson was doing was by asking them, but they often couldn't articulate what they were doing. I've had CEOs approach me to help with sales, and they will tell me they need more salespeople like Mike, their top sales performer. Then, I'll call Mike and say, "Talk to me. Tell me what you're doing on the job to close all of these sales?" In most cases, Mike just says, "I'm doing my job." They likely aren't even fully aware of what they're doing that makes them great, which is why they can't tell you.

This is what makes assessment instruments and observations so great. When we can observe someone, we can understand what methodology they are intuitively following. Interestingly enough, observation is one step on the way to mastery of a skill, so we can use this to determine the training necessary to improve performance. Clients who are interested in this second approach are the clients we can help.

When we use these assessment instruments and observation, we are able to capture unique knowledge from team members specifically relevant to the company itself. Most companies have approximately 57% of their people preparing to retire in the next few years. These are top-performing people who have been there for over 20 years, but what they know often isn't written down anywhere. When we design our trainings, we focus on capturing that legacy knowledge from all of the experienced salespeople so they'll have it forever. Legacy knowledge is everything people on your team know from experience, but it's not written down anywhere. It's everything they ever figured out but never told anyone about. This is one form of peer-to-peer learning we use, and it's extremely effective.

But legacy knowledge doesn't only apply to salespeople who are about to retire. In the current employment environment, it's not unusual for people to change jobs every 18-24 months. Even though these employees may only be with your company for a short amount of time, they bring the experiences from their previous companies and gain unique knowledge about sales for your company that can significantly drive sales. If you can't capture that legacy knowledge from them before they leave, you will be left in the same position you were in before you hired them a year ago.

We capture this legacy knowledge and turn it into training application exercises for each company's sales playbook, so current and new salespeople can refer to how seasoned veterans asked questions and handled objections. These documents and recordings of our virtual training are then prescribed to new employees to shorten their learning curve.

In a recent session, one of the senior-level salespeople at a company shared an amazing question he asks customers, and nobody else on the team had ever heard it before. The messaging was not on the website or in a brochure, and other salespeople were not using it. Everybody on the team immediately asked if they could use it. Absolutely! They can, and they should. Beg, borrow, and steal to get the job done for the good of the company. This type of forced collaboration embedded in my training model can bring out new ideas that can benefit everyone.

Spaced, Stacked Learning

"Learning is not attained by chance, it must be sought for with ardor and diligence."
– Abigail Adams

When I was a trainer at The Timken Company, they sent me to Harvard to improve my management skills. It was an excellent program that included various types of learning, spaced out over time. There was asynchronous learning, which is guided, individual learning; synchronous learning in the form of virtual live sessions and included application exercises and quizzes; and continuous learning opportunities if you wanted more help in a particular skill. It was, by far, one of the best designed training programs I have ever experienced, so much so that I challenged myself to offer this spaced, stacked learning approach in all the training programs I deliver. In one of Harvard's training modules, we learned one of the most effective techniques to train someone is to first identify their skill level, then prescribe training to help them achieve a level of mastery.

Knowing the majority of the off-the-shelf, canned training programs out there are failing their teams, more business owners should be saying, "Screw that!" and use what the data is telling them to deliver a better solution. Why not use a training program designed based on the way adults learn, with little snippets of information, over time, with both asynchronous and synchronous interactions and application exercises?

When we train teams, we first assess for skills gaps, then prescribe training to close those gaps. We design stacked, spaced learning courses designed to stick. We start out by giving participants some information on what we plan to teach them often in an online course, book, article, and/or case study. Next, we do a virtual asynchronous training, reinforcing the key points of emphasis. This part of the training is often an online course they can work through at their own pace and on their own time. Then, we host an online or in-person live training session and have the trainees apply it in an interactive setting. This facilitates peer-to-peer learning and team building as well, which data shows is actually the most effective way of learning.

I am humble enough to admit peer-to-peer learning is much more effective than anything I could do, which is why I incorporate it in my trainings and encourage it often. We role-play common scenarios they face every day so they can practice while receiving coaching and feedback from the instructors and their peers. If we plan to host multiple training sessions, we ask the trainees to do application homework between each session, where they use and apply what they just learned in their day-to-day roles. We prefer to follow virtual training with live instructor-led training and workshops. Here, we reinforce prior skills training, share best practices, and spend the majority of the time practicing the skill safely with their peers, not on customers. Lastly, we assign post-live workshop reinforcement. Here, we leverage online learning to go even deeper into a subject area and recommend books to read.

We often hear business leaders share they want their salespeople to evolve from reps to trusted advisors and industry experts. We just completed this process with a team that sells medical devices. After assessing the team and determining the most common skills gaps, we prescribed online learning for the entire team, while also offering individualized learning for team members who needed other skills not identified on the team report. We held a series of virtual one-hour training sessions with application exercises and delivered a workshop on handling objections and negotiation skills at their national sales meeting. At the end of the meeting, the VP of sales distributed the book *Trusted Advisor* by David Maister to further reinforce why salespeople must evolve based on the changing needs of their buyers. This team now reviews chapters of the book at their monthly sales meetings. I recently spoke with the VP of sales, and his team is now delivering the results he envisioned.

It's important to realize human beings do not learn with one-and-done strategies or death by PowerPoint presentations. Business leaders are often looking for similar results from sales training programs. They want their people to stop relationship-based selling alone and start selling based on value. They want to see an increase in overall gross profit by opening up new accounts and growing market share. It's impossible to achieve these results with a day-and-a-half workshop. They need to build a foundational understanding, learn how to apply what they are learning, demonstrate their level of mastery, and continue to reinforce the skills after the formal training is completed. A good sales training program is taught over a period of time and consists of several components we will discuss in this chapter.

Pre-Learning

"Always walk through life as if you have something new to learn and you will."
– Vernon Howard

No matter which combination of training methods you're using, there should be a pre-learning phase. This happens before the participant ever gets to the training and involves knowledge transfer, where they are exposed to new skills they may never have been trained in before. Pre-learning can take many shapes and forms. You can do it with an online class or by assigning a book, blog posts, or trade journal articles to read. It doesn't matter so much *what* they are doing in advance, so long as it is geared toward preparing them for what's about to happen.

Pre-learning is so important because it is the beginning of the knowledge transfer process and lays the groundwork for everything the participants will learn after. If someone is being exposed to new information for the first time, the pre-learning phase is an easy way to acclimate them to the concepts and material without diving right in and overwhelming them. It also helps to set expectations for what will come next in the learning process. Pre-learning builds exposure to knowledge and lets it soak in overtime before engaging in virtual or instructor-led training or any combination of training styles with application exercises.

Asynchronous Learning

"To unlock the true potential of e-learning to train successful employees, it needs to be people-centered."
– Simon Greany

An asynchronous learning experience is one where the trainee learns instructional material at their own pace and on their own time. We assign asynchronous courses to foster the knowledge transfer initiated in pre-learning and establish an understanding of the content. A strong asynchronous training program typically has quizzes and application exercises and offers more depth in areas where the trainee may want to learn more.

The most important aspect to keep in mind when designing online learning is to make sure it aligns with and builds upon what was done in the pre-learning phase. Your sessions should not introduce a slew of new information not previously covered. Not only will this defeat the point of the knowledge transfer we are building on, but it will also render all of the pre-learning ineffective. There needs to be a correlation the participant can wrap their head around. Suddenly changing the order of how everything connects would cause more confusion than understanding.

When you have an asynchronous program, you need to communicate the goal of the program to the trainees, what we want them to achieve, and by when. They will still do it on their own time and at their own pace, but if you don't set expectations, you run the risk of your trainees not taking the asynchronous learning part seriously. This won't benefit the trainee, just like if they complete the whole training within 12 hours the night before. Asynchronous learning is designed to take place over time.

As the manager overseeing training, you need to watch out for those not participating in asynchronous learning until the night before it's due because they're not getting the benefit out of it. They may open the program, press play, and walk away from their computer. A good online learning system will give you access to how each trainee is progressing through the program including how far they got, how much they complete at a time, and when they last logged in. We have worked with a lot of asynchronous platforms, and we can adapt to any of the ones our clients are currently using, but it's important to find one that works for your goals, objectives, and the industry you're in.

Synchronous Learning

"One of the most important areas we can develop as professionals is competence in accessing and sharing knowledge."
– Connie Malamed

Synchronous learning is live, instructor-led training that can be done virtually or in person. Although it is instructor-led, it is not supposed to be death by PowerPoint. While it may be the easiest format for the subject matter expert to present, it does not deliver the ROI you expect for the time and money invested. The human brain will actually turn off after 90 minutes if not engaged. This is why something as simple as the arrangement of chairs can make a major difference in a learning environment. I've personally never been a fan of arena-themed seating in a classroom, where all the participants sit staring down at the instructor. If you have a smaller group of trainees and a large enough space, consider creating one large circle and have the instructor join the trainees by sitting in that circle or moving around the room. If you have a large group or limited space, one easy approach is to sit people in groups because it's another great opportunity to facilitate peer-to-peer learning. A productive and engaging environment is one where the participants can interact with each other and the facilitator without feeling too formal or rigid.

With all of the great advances in technology, you can host synchronous training sessions over Zoom, Teams, or any other video-based platform. Rather than using death by PowerPoint, learn to utilize all the additional features built into the platform to engage your audience, whether it's breakout rooms, polls, or whiteboards, as well as other learning applications available for free online. Get creative! The more fun you have with facilitating, the more your trainees will engage with and absorb the content.

The Bob Pike Group is a good example of learning and development trainings. They teach that after a certain number of slides in a deck, you need to create an engaging exercise to get the trainees up and participating in some type of activity. The live engagement is all about making them apply the exercise and practice their skills in different everyday scenarios we've identified. We don't want our trainees practicing on customers, so we create a safe environment where salespeople can role-play with their peers. We usually conclude the live engagement session with a project where the trainees practice and demonstrate their skills. Without application and practice, salespeople will be left to try and apply by practicing on your real customers, and that's not good. I ask salespeople to incorporate all the different components of a good sales process and present it to the group, who plays the role of customer.

Data shows the best training is peer-to-peer learning. Your peers have insights and experience with your customers, and we create scenarios for the trainee to apply their negotiation skills in a price increase conversation. They will need to demonstrate how they handle objections. The DISC training can influence how they interact with other personality styles. It's not unusual for us to have everyone in the training program take the DISC assessment ahead of time because the way people sell is dependent on their DISC personality. High Ds have no problem closing sales, whereas high Ss and Cs will typically present the solution and then let the customer come to their own buying decision when they're ready. But each DISC personality also has its strengths so it's important to use them when helping people sell.

Having trainees take the DISC assessment allows the instructor to tailor their facilitation depending on the types of personalities in the room. If we are training a group where the majority of them are high Ds, we can use more bullet points because that is how to most effectively engage a high D audience. However, if the instructor is a high D facilitating to a room of high Ss, they aren't going to be able to rely on those bullet points to engage their audience, and they may need to be aware of the pace at which they are presenting information as well.

During the roleplaying activities, trainees also need to apply their closing skills, all the while the entire class is watching and paying attention. We ask the class for feedback once the exercise is over, so we can discuss:

- What could we have done differently?
- How can we improve?
- Are there strategies you've developed working with clients that could have helped them?

We build that into a sales playbook for existing employees, as well as new ones.

Continuous Learning

"The students of the future will demand the learning support that is appropriate for their situation or context. Nothing more, nothing less. And they want it at the moment the need arises. Not sooner, not later. Mobile devices will be a key technology for providing that learning support."
– Dr. Marcus Specht

Asynchronous training is used to refresh and reinforce through application exercises to go deeper on each subject. Then, synchronous training is where we refresh, reinforce, review quizzes, and spend a little extra time on areas where they've struggled with the quizzes. The instructor is not speaking much in quality, live trainings because the trainees are applying their skills and demonstrating their competence. But training doesn't stop there.

We usually train teams throughout the year, then provide refresher courses for them to take over the next six months to apply their learnings. After that, we go in and facilitate the training again but in different ways. Oftentimes, we will utilize virtual learning for these because it's affordable and easier to schedule, especially if your sales team isn't all located at your headquarters. Not only that, but it takes salespeople away from their role for significantly less time so they can still accomplish what they need to on a daily basis. If a client can't afford an online learning management system, sometimes we'll assign books for people to read and use for virtual engagements. I like to have people read articles I've personally written or watch videos from industry experts.

Mastery

"To become a master at any skill, it takes the total effort of your: heart, mind, and soul working together in tandem."
–Maurice Young

Mastery is a new term to many of my clients. Many of them made a career for themselves in financial operations, and now they're running a company, so the whole training experience is just a black box to them. They don't understand it, but what they do know is it's expensive and it doesn't work. They're not wrong though because the whole system is broken, which is why I designed a training program to work.

The goal of any training program is not only to turn an unskilled employee into someone who now has the tools to do their job effectively but also to help those who are proficient reach a level of mastery. There are going to be critics out there who believe mastery can be gained from an online course, but I personally don't believe it, and I've never experienced it in all my years doing this. Can someone become skilled through virtual learning alone? Sure, but they're unlikely to become a master at it.

The best way to tell if a skill has been learned is if it can be demonstrated. For me, this would make a person skilled. They took what they learned and put it into practice without any oversight. Any of these training methods can be combined to deliver the result of knowledge transfer. Mastery, however, is when someone can take the skill they just learned and successfully teach someone else how to do it themselves. Even the most seasoned and skilled salespeople might not rise to the level of mastery because they are unable to help anyone else get to their level. There is nothing wrong with this distinction for your regular salesforce, but when taking into consideration who should get promoted to leadership or management, the mastery level should become a determining factor.

We want to develop our teams to different levels so not everyone is in the same place at the same time. A novice won't become a master in 12 months, but they can become skilled, and skilled people can evolve into masters. If you visualize a bell curve, typically 10%-20% of the team requires a lot of help. 60% of the team is moderate, right in the middle, and the remaining 20% are top performers. Everyone wants to turn their worst performers into the best, but when it comes to training, my advice is to move that middle part of the bell curve representing 60% of your team. The results to your bottom line will be exponential.

I want to leave you with one cautionary word of advice when it comes to training your team – a lot of instructors go into training with the wrong expectations. About 20% of the people you train don't want to be there, and they're not going to engage. They only went because you made them or because it is a paid day out of the office. There isn't much you can do for these people, but the other 80% need your help. Don't compromise your model based on the 20% that might not even be a good fit for your organization. Train your teams based on what gaps the assessment exercise revealed need closing. If the 20% can't be trained or coached, then meet with their managers and discuss other roles within the organization or a plan for transitioning them out of the company altogether.

Chapter 7: Execution

"Feedback on performance should be immediate, built into operating procedures, and fact-based. It should address specific actions and events, not personality."
– Michael Armstrong & Angela Baron

You've just spent the last six chapters diligently taking notes and creating a plan to help your team improve their sales performance. Now, it's time to put the book down and get to work on generating revenue, right? Not so fast. From my experience, it is always best to create a tracking system used to ensure everyone in your organization is performing to the original plan. Most teams will go through the whole process and get the short-term motivation to put everything they have learned into action. Sadly, as time goes by, they fall right back into the way they've always done things.

It comes as a shock to some of my clients, but the last thing I want to happen is for them to come back and hire me again in 12-18 months to address the same issues. I want to help you create a system and process where you can stay on top of the behaviors and processes yourself. Sure, they can always call me back if a new situation arises, but I don't want them investing more money to fix a problem we already addressed. To ensure you are able to achieve the same level of independence in your business, we are going to cover some key areas of execution in this chapter.

KPIs

"If you can't measure it, you can't improve it."
– Peter Drucker

When you teach someone a new skill that isn't then reinforced and monitored, they will regress back to what they were doing before. One way to prevent this is to measure what matters by establishing relevant key performance indicators (KPIs). While businesses may have many performance indicators and metrics, they should only have a few KPIs, which are outputs of success. It's important to establish these measurements, and they need to be leading and lagging indicators. A leading indicator is an action or behavior that could result in an outcome, while a lagging indicator is something that has already happened like a completed sale, shipment, or meeting. We need to track and measure both of these if we want the plan to be executed successfully. To do this, our actions must align with our plan and our objectives, and the team should be trying the new skills we recommended.

This process is very much like learning to fly an airplane. One of the first things you learn when you take flight lessons is how to use and trust the various instruments in the plane. When you get thousands of feet in the air, it is easy to lose sight of where you came from, so those instruments are designed to keep you on track. One of the most powerful instruments for a business, particularly when it comes to scaling up and growing your sales, is your Customer Relationship Management system, or CRM. A good CRM has dashboards designed to advance sales by tracking your KPIs, which include the leading and lagging indicators to compare what happened in the past to what could lead to a sale in the future.

Lagging indicators pertain to what happened in the past and some examples are:
- What were last month's sales?
- What were last month's profits?
- How many new accounts did we add last month?

Some leading indicators are:
- How many prospects were reached out to?
- How many meetings were booked?
- How many prospects were sent quotes?
- How many deals in the sales pipeline advance to the next phase?

Some common KPIs (that will vary by industry):

- On-time shipments
- Quality-based parts per million
- Invoices outstanding
- Manufacturing variance

As we scale companies, we should have KPIs for every department and post the results somewhere easily accessible for the team to see. The best way to ensure compliance with the plan is to monitor those KPIs. If someone is drifting off plan, we need to coach them back into compliance. If someone is consistently not complying with the new process or CRM, we may find we are actually coaching a mindset issue.

For example, we often work with sales teams that need to evolve from quoting based on what it costs to make it versus what the market value is. To sell based on value, salespeople need to establish value early in the sales process. A phone call and a quote without discovery or qualifying aren't practicing value-based selling. We have to quickly correct the behaviors we observe that are out of alignment with the plan, but we can only do that by using specific performance metrics for each role throughout our organization. When we plan to have sales teams set prices based on value, not cost, we monitor metrics in the Enterprise Resource Planning (ERP) system or wherever they store transaction data. We look at sales, the margin per sale, the overall account blended margin, and so on.

To ensure compliance, we will typically develop a strategic plan where we decide on what our "big rocks" are, or the things that significantly impact our business, as Covey describes them. Each leader meets with their teams and develops the key activities their teams need to do to achieve this objective. Then, each leader meets with their team members individually and asks what they feel they need to do to impact the business's overall objectives. We establish the KPIs with each team member, monitor them, and use the Foursquare model discussed in Chapter 5 to keep things moving.

Discipline

"Discipline is not the same as hierarchical obedience or adherence to bureaucratic rules. True discipline requires the independence of mind to reject pressure and conform in ways incompatible with value and performance standards, as well as the inner will to do what it takes to create a great outcome."
– Jim Collins & Morten Hansen

Discipline is all about doing the right things, even when it gets hard. Some people refer to this as grit. We need to take the right approach to help our teams continue down the right path with appropriate activities and be prepared to support them when they get stuck. It's crucial for them to show up with discipline day after day to perform the activities they've signed up for, helped contribute to, and executed on.

I was blessed to learn discipline in my martial arts training. We practiced over and over again, constantly refining our techniques. Our instructors made adjustments to our hand position, foot movement, breathing, and speed. We practiced so often that we built muscle memory. Although we were not aware of it until we achieved upper-belt rank, our goal was to practice so much, so often, and correctly, that should an opportunity to use this technique occur, we would act without thought – what we referred to as Mushin or no mind. Our bodies would respond without hesitation, thought, or fear. We applied these techniques in controlled scenarios and when sparring with others. Eventually, we advanced in belt rank and taught the new students. This was a brilliant model to develop and demonstrate mastery when you have to teach a skill.

We need that same discipline in our businesses. The best-performing teams prospect continuously. The quickest way I can determine if a team is not prospecting continuously is by looking at their revenue by month and monitoring their prospecting activities. Poor-performing sales teams have trends that resemble a rollercoaster. They have a great month and then a terrible month, which is a symptom of a team not prospecting continuously. When I work with a team like that, I ask the sales leaders to show me their prospecting log. I want to see the dashboard activity in their CRM that shows who they're talking with every week about their prospecting activities. Normally, that's the root of the problem. You need to have dashboards that monitor the key behaviors your team needs to do in their particular roles to drive maximum performance. These dashboards don't need to be anything fancy, just functional enough to show where you stand at a glance on the top 3-5 KPIs you are tracking.

Performance Reviews

"Performance management involves embracing employees' strengths and being open to innovative ideas – even ones that change the status quo."
– Steve Jobs

Many companies that experience difficulties in their operations tend to implement a yearly performance review process often lacking balance and fairness. During these reviews, it's common for the manager to solely provide the employees with a report card, outlining their strengths and weaknesses, without any engaging feedback or input from the employee. This process is detrimental to the overall growth and developmental needs of both the company and the employee, as it lacks a collaborative effort toward improvement.

On the contrary, market-leading companies place significant emphasis on conducting regular and thorough performance evaluations, generally on a quarterly basis, and they use the Foursquare model we spoke about earlier. This model involves assessing the progress made by employees toward achieving their goals, so companies can optimize their workforce, improve overall performance, and maintain a competitive edge in the market.

Performance reviews offer a unique opportunity to comprehensively evaluate employee performance and strategically pinpoint areas of strength and those needing improvement. These reviews are an invaluable tool for both employees and managers when fostering professional development and creating an environment of trust and safety. Managers can offer personalized training opportunities tailored to meet their unique needs and promote continuous improvement. Through honest and open communication, employees can confidently discuss their goals, strengths, and weaknesses. Eliciting input and feedback from employees allows managers to craft a realistic and rewarding plan of action.

Quarterly reviews also offer several advantages for teams to stay agile and adaptable. Regular assessments of progress and making adjustments every few months allow for small changes that lead to significant results over time. Companies conducting more frequent performance evaluations have higher employee engagement, performance, and retention rates. In contrast, teams that only conduct annual reviews can lose a substantial amount of time that could be better spent proactively addressing issues and opportunities. The ultimate goal of the performance review process is to provide the employee with a clear and comprehensive understanding of how their performance is being evaluated and what they can do to improve in areas where they may be struggling.

During my performance review meetings, I consistently delve into career planning. There is one instance I recall where I sat down with a young salesperson who confidently expressed his desire to hold the same job position as myself, VP of Sales. Intrigued by his ambition, we mapped out a plan of action to help him achieve his aspirations. Together, we began identifying relevant courses and training programs that would equip him with the necessary skills and knowledge to excel in his role and eventually transition into a higher position. I also provided him with books to expand his industry expertise and offered extra coaching to further develop his leadership abilities. Although he ultimately moved on from the company, he is now a successful VP of Sales at a leading manufacturing firm. This goes to show how performance reviews, when conducted properly, can bring out the hidden potential of the people in your organization.

When evaluating an employee's performance, I consider several factors. While it is crucial they meet their numerical targets, their approach to achieving these goals is equally significant. I look at whether they have followed our company's culture or have chosen to bypass our established systems. We do not want a workforce that solely consists of high-achieving individuals but who have behaviorally challenging traits.

At my core, I believe every individual has the potential to achieve greatness. However, we often find some individuals may not perform at an optimal level due to a mismatch between their skills, the culture they're immersed in, or being placed in the wrong role altogether. As a leader, my first step when identifying these individuals is to offer coaching and training opportunities to help them grow and become more productive. Despite these efforts, we have come across a segment of individuals who are unwilling to be coached or trained, showing a clear reluctance towards changing their current approach or attitude. These individuals refuse to do what's necessary for their assigned role and pose a hindrance to the organization's progress. It is our responsibility to identify and address this barrier by coaching them out of the organization.

When it comes to the decision of firing employees, it should always be viewed as a last resort. This drastic measure should only be taken if the company's finances are in a dire state or if all other options for employee development have failed. Unfortunately, in many cases, especially among large companies, the focus is mainly on the stock value, and the strategy adopted to improve the stock value is to cut down on the workforce. This can have severe implications for employees and the overall growth of the company.

As a young manager, I was faced with the challenge of firing an employee who, in my opinion, did not deserve to lose their job. The decision to terminate their employment came as a complete surprise to both the employee and myself, but it came from what I call "mount high," or a higher level of management than myself, so I was left with no choice but to follow through. The experience left me with a lot of personal anxiety, numerous sleepless nights, and a host of digestive problems, as I found it difficult to cope with the stress of the situation.

I have been on the other side of the table as well. After dedicating my time and effort to assist companies in their growth, I've come to accept that sometimes, things don't always align perfectly. I've found myself in situations where a new owner takes over, and unfortunately, I'm no longer the right fit for the company's vision. My entrepreneurial spirit drove me to passionately pursue growth and development, and if the new ownership did not share the same values and ambitions, it became a challenging obstacle. While I've sometimes been let go in a respectful and mutual way that allowed for a smooth transition, other times have been more of a rough and frustrating experience.

During a meeting with a newly appointed CEO, he tactfully acknowledged the current situation wasn't the best fit for me because the company had a different vision from what I was used to when they acquired the enterprise. He presented me with a question: Could I adjust my style and continue to run the business, or would I consistently maintain my current hard-driving approach? After some contemplation, I affirmed I would always have the same drive. The CEO seemed to have expected this response, but he showed great professionalism and offered a helping hand. He suggested I start seeking new opportunities and gave me a generous three-month period to prepare for my departure. I found the entire experience to be eye-opening, as it enabled me to review my life choices and seek better opportunities. The best part is, the CEO and I remained friends despite all the changes that occurred.

Then, there were times when being fired did not feel so good. I was brought in by the company to turn their sales around after experiencing a staggering 30% drop. Despite their initial concerns about needing to let employees go, I was able to add 285 new customers in just 18 months, causing the business to thrive. In fact, they had to open a second shift to handle the increase in demand. Nonetheless, one day, a family member, accompanied by human resources, came into my office and informed me it was my last day working there. They refused to give a reason, stating they were not legally required to do so, and collected my laptop and phone. When I asked about an exit plan, there was none. I later discovered my termination was due to the company's desire to cut costs, despite the strong and continuing growth I had helped to generate. It seems all the new accounts and new orders generated challenges for another family member running production. That family member felt we had "enough" business, and my services were no longer needed.

The heart of any organization lies in its people, and when they perform well, the organization thrives. That's why the use of performance reviews is crucial to promote execution in an organization. However, it's not just about evaluating employees based on their job performance. It's about providing constructive feedback that inspires them to grow and excel. Performance reviews should focus on specific goals and areas of improvement, leading to a culture of continuous learning and development. They should also be a two-way conversation, giving employees an opportunity to share their thoughts on the organization's strategies and goals. When done well, performance reviews can ignite a fire in employees, fostering a deep sense of commitment and engagement in the organization's success.

Incentive Plans

"An incentive is a bullet, a key: an often tiny object with astonishing power to change a situation."
– Steven Levitt

Organizations have long relied on incentive plans to inspire their employees to perform their duties with maximum efficiency and effectiveness. These plans take the form of targeted compensation, designed to reward employees upon achieving specific goals, milestones, or objectives set by the organization. Because incentive plans serve as a powerful catalyst for helping employees to maintain focus, motivation, and commitment, their significance to promote execution within an organization cannot be overstated.

The implementation of incentive plans can enhance the execution and overall success of an organization by aligning individual goals with the company's objectives. Incentive plans provide a clear understanding to employees of the importance of their roles in achieving the organization's objectives, which instills a stronger sense of commitment, drive, and focus to better execute their personal duties. When employees are aligned with the organization's objectives through incentive plans, they work harder and smarter toward achieving the set goals. This approach results in enhanced productivity levels and improved quality of work, ultimately leading to the successful execution of projects and initiatives.

Incentive plans can also create a sense of urgency in employees, compelling them to put forth extra effort and work harder to achieve their objectives. Knowing they can be rewarded is a powerful motivator, leading to greater job satisfaction and dedication to the company. When incentivized appropriately, employees are more likely to take ownership of their goals by investing more time and energy in achieving them, leading to faster project execution and greater returns on investment for the organization.

There is also a way to use incentive plans to establish a culture of healthy competition within an organization. When employees realize they are competing with their colleagues to achieve specific targets, they often become motivated to work harder. A culture of performance-driven competition among employees enhances individual employee performance and aligns the entire organization toward achieving its broader objectives. By providing these incentives, an organization demonstrates its commitment to promoting employee excellence and encourages everyone to continuously strive for success.

Offering incentive plans can also be an excellent tool for organizations to retain employees who consistently perform at a high level. It rewards employees for going above and beyond in their work, engages and motivates the workforce, and drives organizational culture. When employees feel valued and appreciated, they become more committed to delivering the necessary output to accomplish the organization's objectives.

As a firm believer in a targeted compensation model, I ensure each role in my organization has a compensation package based on the market price for that particular role. However, I always strive to pay my team members slightly higher than the industry rate, mainly because I hold them to very high standards and expect exceptional outcomes from them. During the performance review process, my team members are fully aware of what their future compensation plans, bonuses, and commissions entail. There are no surprises when we discuss all pertinent details, leaving little room for confusion or misunderstanding. If an employee is ever surprised by a lower-than-expected salary increase at the end of the year, it indicates a lack of effective communication between the manager and the employee and a failure of the performance review process.

To manage my compensation process effectively, managers are allocated budgets to distribute salary increases based on performance. Managers will usually prioritize their high-performing employees, followed by those who are performing satisfactorily. Unfortunately, employees who do not meet the expected standards may be counseled out of the organization or encouraged to leave. Adopting this approach has allowed me to create a cohesive work environment that clearly outlines what is expected from each team member, all while providing fair and competitive compensation packages in line with industry standards. This has resulted in a team that is motivated, committed, and determined to exceed expectations repeatedly, resulting in tremendous business success.

Technology

"Technology is a useful servant but a dangerous master."
– Christian Lous Lange

We each have so many activities going on in both our personal and professional lives on a daily basis that it can be difficult to prioritize and manage. The flip side of this fast-paced existence includes all of the technologies designed for us to perform these tasks and track progress. We now have a phone app for almost anything you can think about, and the desktop and web-based programs available to businesses are even more sophisticated. Not all options will be relevant for all industries, company sizes, or situations, but taking the time to figure out which ones can be the most beneficial for your business will help save time, reduce costs, and improve efficiency over time.

CRM

Your Customer Relationship Management (CRM) becomes your single voice of truth when used correctly and can be used as one of your measurement tools to advance sales. I could probably spend an entire chapter on all things CRM related, but that's not the point of this book. Your CRM helps you to gather insights and store them all in one place. It's imperative to avoid turning your salespeople into librarians, looking through mountains and mountains of information instead of engaging with their customers. There are hundreds, if not thousands, of options, and the decision on which is the right one for you boils down to the one that has the most features you will find value in.

Anytime you buy anything, particularly in the technology space, it is a best practice to first understand your requirements and the job you need it to do for the investment to be worthwhile. A higher-priced option is not always better than a lower-priced option if you will be paying for a lot of features you don't need.

Project Management

Project management software is a highly valuable tool in assisting management to support execution by breaking down complex projects into smaller, more manageable tasks. This enables team members to be assigned specific tasks that align with their skills, capabilities, and availability. With the ability to track progress, management has an informed view of what tasks are outstanding and who is responsible for each task. This powerful feature alone ensures projects stay on track, with everything being completed on time.

Asana and Trello are two project management tools for projects of all sizes. They provide a dashboard view of progress, status, and who within the organization is accountable for each task. This allows for streamlined communication and collaboration between team members, helping to reduce the risk of delays and misunderstandings. Managers can also track the time spent on each task, which enables them to monitor team progress, identify any issues, and resolve them in a timely manner.

Communication

With advancements in technology, various communication software such as Slack or Microsoft Teams have emerged as tools for streamlining team communication and increasing productivity. By facilitating instant messaging, file sharing, and collaborative workspaces, these platforms eliminate the possibility of ambiguity or misunderstandings that can hinder progress. These tools also offer a range of other benefits, such as:

- allowing remote teams to work collaboratively.
- reducing travel expenses.
- providing team members with more flexibility.
- offering users features, such as task lists and shared calendars, so everyone is aware of deadlines and responsibilities.

With the ability to keep everyone in the organization on the same page, these tools assist in coordinating and optimizing workflows, resulting in increased productivity and efficiency. Businesses that embrace these technologies are likely to stay ahead of the curve and outperform those that do not.

Automation

Using software to automate routine tasks enables us to save precious time and focus on other higher-value activities. Applications like Zapier or IFTTT can significantly expedite your workflows by easily automating manual tasks. Automating tasks can eliminate error-prone manual processes and focus on more value-added tasks. Additionally, software automation offers considerable benefits such as 24/7 availability and scalability. It can improve the productivity of your team and increase customer satisfaction through faster, more efficient services.

Security

One of the most significant advantages of software programs is the ability to reduce downtime caused by unforeseen circumstances. Advanced cybersecurity software can detect and mitigate potential threats, ensuring confidential data stays safe and secure. Similarly, antivirus software protects company systems from malicious viruses and malware, aiding in the seamless execution of various processes. By leveraging security software, businesses can maintain a high level of operational efficiency while avoiding the severe consequences of downtime. The implementation of software to mitigate risks associated with cyber threats and viruses is a crucial step toward safeguarding the interests of the organization and its stakeholders, making the investment into advanced software solutions a prudent decision for business owners who seek to reduce downtime and ensure the continuous execution of business operations.

Analysis

Leveraging software analysis tools can also help management achieve organizational success by providing insights on critical metrics. With the help of business intelligence software, crucial information such as website traffic, customer engagement, and order fulfillment rates can be tracked and analyzed to optimize business processes. By utilizing these insights, management can tailor their marketing strategies to attract potential customers and retain existing ones, thereby enhancing the overall customer experience. In addition, the data can also inform strategic resource allocation, ensuring company resources are effectively allocated for maximum efficiency and growth.

ERP

Enterprise Resource Planning (ERP) systems are, without a doubt, invaluable in streamlining team activities and enhancing execution. Centralized databases ensure all critical information is stored away, easily accessible, and effectively managed. Thanks to their reliance on ERP systems, teams can minimize errors, maximize efficiency, and ensure clear communication between different departments. Adopting an integrated approach, ERP systems handle numerous processes from procurement and production to distribution. By leveraging innovative ERP technology, teams can work with the utmost accuracy and speed, ultimately delivering top-quality products to their clients.

This high degree of automation empowers manufacturing teams to function seamlessly, with each process flowing into the next. By providing real-time data, ERP systems empower teams to closely monitor the progress of production, analyze both historical and future trends, and efficiently schedule production activities and capacity. With the integrated tools provided by the systems, manufacturing teams can make informed decisions in real-time to increase efficiency and productivity.

Chapter 8: Putting It All Together

"For something to be innovative it needs to offer new functionality (technical insight), but it also has to be surprising to the user. Give consumers something they had no idea existed and solve a problem that they will only find out about tomorrow."
– Peter Senge & George Roth

As we get ready to wrap everything up, give yourself a pat on the back. You made it all the way to the end of the book and hopefully have tons of notes and actionable steps you can start putting into place in your own business. I am not going to bore anyone by repeating all the content or summarizing the key takeaways. As a business owner, it's important to understand profitable, sustainable businesses don't just spring up overnight, and the ones fortunate enough to reach that level are not guaranteed to stay there. They are strategically developed. This holds true whether you're a startup company that has identified an unmet market need or you're a leader or an owner of an existing company that's been around for 100 years.

I have shared a framework to help you launch your business, grow your existing business, launch into new markets, and acquire new customers. The process has worked for me for over 30 years and has helped hundreds, if not thousands, of clients. The people I have trained have undoubtedly paid it forward. So long as you follow the process, it is impossible not to be successful, but I want to remind you I did not create any of this on my own. I went out, did research, read books, attended seminars and conferences, and sought to become an expert. This is what I recommend all leaders do – have an insatiable hunger to learn about the area they are in. Doing so has helped me find some amazing content my clients could use to grow profitably. As I shared when we started this journey together – there is nothing new under the sun. However, there are always new ways to apply wisdom.

Throughout this book, you should have noticed I have promoted other people's books and recommended you buy them and engage with the authors. If you're asking yourself why, the answer is simple – because I know it will make a difference for you and your team. I've applied it more times than I can count, and I've shown you how I've applied it. Maybe you're going to apply this knowledge in different ways, and that's okay. There are thousands and thousands of books out there you can read; I'm simply sharing the ones I've already used or am going to use to address the ever-changing market needs of our customers.

In the resource section to follow, I have provided you with a QR code to the website where you can find all the resources mentioned throughout the book and the list of all the different books, seminars, and powerful companies you can work with to help your company profitably scale and increase shareholder value.

My mission in writing this book is to help people have a framework they can apply to make their visions and dreams come true. No business has to remain stagnant if the will and skill exist to fix it. Businesses evolve, they change, they pivot, and they are faced with new constraints every day. In 2022, one of the biggest constraints was supply chain, and many companies had to evolve or they risked going out of business. In 2023, there are new situations emerging that have a direct impact on our businesses, and this will happen again in 2024, 2025, and so on.

As Jim Collins said in his book *How The Mighty Fall: And Why Some Companies Never Give In,* "Every institution is vulnerable, no matter how great it is. Anyone can fail. Institutional decline happens in five stages: Hubris Born of Success, Undisciplined Pursuit of More, Denial of Risk and Peril, Grasping for Salvation, and Capitulation to Irrelevance or Death. A crisis can be prevented if declining systems are detected in time. As long as a company has not reached the fifth, terminal stage, decline can be reversed. Don't overestimate your own merit and capabilities. Luck and chance play a role in many successful outcomes."

If you follow this process, you're going to have insights into the shifts and pivots in your customers' buying behavior, your markets, new market needs that many of your competitors are going to miss, and an abundance of other useful information. The data you need is out there. The only question is, "What you are going to do with it?"

Epilogue

When I work with clients or when I speak at events I often refer to the work I do with clients as my "ministry." What do I mean by that?

This is my way of giving back and thanking all of those who invested in training and coaching me over the years. It's my way of helping others and making the world a better place.

When I was in my late 20s and early 30s, I was considered "successful" by the world's standards – not super wealthy but well off. I had a generous compensation package, stock options, a beautiful house, nice vacations, an imported car, and a lake house with a boat for weekend getaways. I had a wife and two beautiful, gifted children. I was helping my company grow over 20% year over year. I traveled four nights a week and often worked Saturdays to catch up. We had so much success growing revenues in North America I was asked to launch international sales. Within two years, international sales grew to exceed $20 million, but I was traveling three weeks per month, leaving my wife and children at home to create a life without me.

No matter how many more sales I made or how much I helped our team grow market share or increase profits, it never filled the hole inside my chest. My expensive imported car spent more time in the airport parking garage than being driven. One evening, I was working on a proposal from a recent trip to Japan, and my young son came into my home office, wanting to get my attention and spend time with me since I had been gone for weeks. He tried many times to win my attention and eventually pushed over a stack of papers. I screamed, "No!" and he ran out of the room crying.

I felt terrible. I ran after him and asked, "Why are you crying?"

I will never forget what he said next – "You look at me with mean eyes."

My heart broke. The intensity and drive I had to grow businesses were hurting the relationships I had with my family. The family I justified working so hard for. At that moment, I knew I needed to change. I tried a number of things: I hired a coach, attended self-help seminars on a balanced life, read piles of books, and even looked into Buddhism based on the suggestion of my martial arts instructor. Though it was interesting, it did not seem to help.

One day, while picking my son up from preschool at the local church, I bumped into the minister in the hallway. He casually asked, "Why the long face?" I thought, *What could it hurt? This guy is a stranger.* So, I unloaded my burdens. He shared that the empty place I had been trying to fill with growing a business, having a big home, and fancy cars would never be filled without a relationship with Jesus.

I thought to myself, *I tried everything else, so why not?*

He invited me to a course they offered every Wednesday evening called Alpha. It was like a Christianity 101 course. We met, had a nice dinner, watched a video recording, and discussed each topic. There were no right or wrong answers. As I answered questions, it made me want to have a relationship with Jesus and ask Him into my life…so I did. I wish I could say everything in my life changed for the better overnight, but it didn't. I actually experienced some major life disruptions as I tried to apply these faith-based principles to every aspect of my life.

Fast forward to today. I have led Alpha programs where I introduced over 40 churches and 30-80 people to Christ. Each day, I spend time in God's word and journal. I pray before each keynote speech, saying, "Lord, help me help someone in the audience. Speak through me." Before each client engagement, I pray, "Lord, help me help this leadership team and company grow and better serve their customers and their community." I pray for the leaders I work with and their families. With some of my faith-based clients, I pray with them and attend their Bible studies before work when I am in their town.

Why am I sharing this in my book on driving explosive growth?

My purpose, my *why,* for continuing to help companies is to find busy, high-performing executives who, like me, have that all-too-familiar hole in their chests. When I do, which is often, I share how becoming a Christ follower has helped me.

If you read my book, and it helps your business drive explosive growth, it would make all my years of training and learning the hard way worthwhile. The reason I invested in being a Scaling Up coach is so it can help business leaders work fewer hours and get greater results while having more time for their faith, family, health, and friends.

My faith journey is just that – a journey. Each day, I learn new things, and my relationship with Jesus grows stronger. If you find success is not enough, and you wish or need to have a deeper sense of meaning and serve others, please reach out and I would enjoy helping you on your faith journey as much, if not more, than on your business growth journey.

God Bless,

Mark

Resources

For continued learning on any of the topics we covered in this book, don't forget to head over to my website using the QR code below. If you are struggling with a constraint like time or doing this all alone seems daunting, don't hesitate to reach out to me directly for a free consultation on the ways we can work together to drive explosive growth in your business.

Acknowledgments

Harry Jones, my first manager at Frito-Lay, who encouraged, trained, and coached me to be a sales leader.

Jim Sankey, who taught me how to find unresolved market problems and turn them into products to serve our customers.

Verne Harnish, author of the book *Scaling Up* and the entire Scaling Up coaches' support team.

Matt from Penforhire, who, without his framework and methodology, this book would not have been possible.

All my clients who have asked me to serve them and, in each experience, taught me so much.

Alpha USA, the program that led me to want a relationship with Jesus.

Bill and Roxanne Marcum, my martial arts instructors who taught me discipline and gave me a framework to teach others.

To the thousands of authors and thought leaders who I have read and who have gifted me with the knowledge to serve others and help them make their dreams come true in business and their personal lives.

45402040R00089